The Canadian Nights

by

Katharine Campbell

To Meg,
I hope this
makes you
laugh,

ISBN: 978-1-09838-704-4 (print)
ISBN: 978-1-09838-705-1 (eBook)

To Joe,

who always appreciates my unfiltered sense of humor.

Contents

Amala is Abducted by Canadians

The president of the United States has a giant red button on his desk. If he ever chose to push this button, it would send the world into chaos. There would be global panic, revolutions, rioting in the streets. This button is for emergencies only and is designed to break the internet.

How do I know this button exists? *Please.* Everyone knows it exists.

In our universe, this button has never been pushed. But ours is not the only universe. There is another universe, almost exactly like our own. That universe also has a United States, and a president with a giant red button on her desk. It is a world so much like our own, that if you accidentally stumbled into it, you wouldn't notice the difference. At least, not at first. After a time, you might notice some minor differences. For example, there are no fantasy creatures in this parallel world, because every creature that we consider fictional, actually exists. There are a few extra countries on the map, and the folks in Chicago like ketchup on their hotdogs. I call this other universe Para Sympan, which of course comes from the ancient Helivinian *Para* (Second) and *Sympan* (World).

If you are thinking that there is no such language as Helivinian, you are right. There isn't in our universe. Helevinia is a country in Para Sympan.

Of course, the most relevant difference between our universe and Para Sympan is that in Para Sympan, the giant red button on the president's desk *was* pushed. The consequences were horrific.

It all started because a house cleaner in the Oval Office noticed some mold on the inside of the glass case that covered the button. Now, technically, to remove the glass for cleaning and maintenance, you need to get approval by filling out a form, driving to the correct state department, waiting in line for four hours to submit the form to a human agent, wait while the agent retypes the information into the computer, then wait at least six weeks for the information to be reviewed.

The house cleaner decided to speed things up by skipping the paperwork and removing the glass herself. Unfortunately, her finger slipped.

At that very moment, Canadian prime minister, Liam Champagne, was sitting in his lodge streaming the hockey game. Now, Canadians are known for being mild-mannered; that is because they vent all their violent tendencies by watching hockey. The Canadian prime minister called the president to ask her to restore service.

The president had been golfing when the internet went down. She did not realize anything was wrong until her butler, Blaine, appeared carrying a red rotary telephone on a velvet pillow.

"Prime Minister Champagne, madam," he droned.

"Who?" The president questioned.

"The prime minister of Canada," Blaine replied.

"Canada?" she asked.

"The country up north," Blaine continued.

She still seemed a bit confused.

"The place where moose live, madam."

"Oh, right!" She snatched the handset.

"Y'ello?" she said.

"Oh, hey there," Minister Champagne started. "I was er . . . just wondering if you hit that internet kill switch?"

The president cupped her hand over the mouthpiece and looked up at Blaine. "Does our base like Canada?"

"Let me check the forums, madam," Blaine replied. He pulled out his smart phone and spent a somber moment scrolling. "The internet seems to be down, madam. But it may interest you to know that, if my memory serves me, Mister Champagne was once photographed with Governor Jenkins at a Tim Hortons."

Governor Jenkins was part of the *other* party. The bad party. The party that wasn't the president's party. (You know which party I am talking about.)

She took her hand off the mouthpiece, "What if I did?" she asserted.

"Erm, could you, ah, please turn the internet back on?" The prime minister requested.

"Why don't you come up here?" The president started.

"*Down* here, madam," Blaine interrupted. "Canada is north."

"*Down* here and make me!"

"Hey, there's a hockey game goin', and folks up here are beginin' to get all unruly and outta sorts."

"That's your problem," the president replied and hung up. She grinned at Blaine. "Not going to let Canada walk all over me."

W ithout hockey to vent their aggression, the Canadians snapped. They stopped saying please and thank you. They started pushing past people without saying excuse me, and even started littering. It was a disaster. The prime minister himself was feeling a bit put out. In desperation, he ordered that all US citizens on Canadian soil be arrested.

He then called the president and told her that every night that she didn't restore the internet, he was going to have one US citizen dipped in maple syrup and thrown to a horde of angry beavers.

Now despite the prime minister's horrific threat, the president would not reactivate the internet. No matter how many US citizens were mauled by beavers, she stood firm. Politicians in the opposing party (you know which party I'm talking about) thought about sneaking into her office and reactivating the internet themselves, but they realized that the crisis was making her look bad, and since there was another election coming up, they allowed it to continue.

So it was that many ordinary people were caught in the middle of an ugly political conflict. One such person was Amala Patel. She lived in Santa Clara and had taken a road trip up the coast into British Columbia for spring break. She was riding a moose through a Tim Hortons drive-through when the news broke, and shortly thereafter, a couple of Mounties politely asked her to come with them.

She was taken to Ottawa, where she was treated horribly. The police confined her to a two-star hotel. The coffee was burnt, and the only condiments they had were powdered creamer and sugar replacement. Every evening, everyone was brought to the lobby which smelled like cigarette smoke and was covered in dusty, taxidermied animals. There was an old TV with a VCR attached in the corner. A curling instructional video from 1995 was always playing.

(Some readers may be deeply disturbed by the description above, but I feel it's necessary to document the awful tortures the Canadians inflicted.)

While gathered in that awful lobby, the prime minister himself would arrive and personally select his next victim.

Now, Amala was a selfless soul, and during her confinement, she only thought of her fellow prisoners and how she could save them and bring the entire conflict to an end. Without the internet, she had plenty of time to think. She formulated a plan.

That evening when the prime minister arrived, Amala spoke up immediately.

"Pick me next," she exclaimed.

Everyone looked at her in stunned silence.

"Oh wow, that's really nice of you," Minister Champagne responded. "Are you sure?"

"Absolutely! I would rather die than have to drink another cup of Stuart's coffee."

Stuart, the hotel manager, was a greasy gorilla of a man. He glared at her from behind the reception desk.

"Oh! Don't be silly," Champagne replied. "You're not gonna die. But you will need a tetanus shot for all the beaver bites. And you'll have to pay for it yourself after we throw you back over the border."

As awful as paying for her own tetanus shot sounded, Amala was brave and committed to her plan.

"Before you throw me to the beavers, can I make one last request?"

"Oh yeah, for sure," Champagne nodded.

"Everyone's tired of watching that curling tape."

"We have a hiking safety instructional video under the couch," Stuart interjected from behind the registration desk. "Oh, and the first half of *Titanic*." He held aloft a VHS tape.

Amala's fellow captives groaned.

"Thanks, but I think I'd just like to tell a story," she answered.

"Whatever floats your boat," the prime minister answered with a shrug. He took a seat on a taxidermied cougar and sent his assistant to the car for a beer.

The following is the story that Amala told.

2

The Dual at Mackerel Valley Airport

not one of the fifty thousand employees that worked at the Mackerel
Valley International Airport were happy. In fact, two were down-
right miserable. Their names were Troy and Janice. They were gate
agents, and they hated each other.

The rivalry started shortly after they both began. By complete coincidence,
they were hired at the same time, started on the same day, and assigned to
adjacent gates. When they started working, their planes arrived around the same
time and were ready to board shortly after.

Janice picked up her intercom handset a moment before Troy and
announced: "Welcome to Intermittent Airlines flight 1300—"

But she was cut off by Troy's announcement echoing through the speakers
in his gate area.

It was the standard Intermittent Airlines pre-boarding announcement:

"Welcome to Intermittent Airlines Flight 666 with service to Fish City,
Pennsylvania. Because you were either too cheap or too afraid to check your

baggage, we are going to have to do it by force. If you prefer not to have it wrestled out of your hands by one of our flight attendants, please come to the podium to surrender it peacefully. We will begin boarding shortly."

Janice finished making the same announcement a few moments later.

When it actually came time to board the flight, Janice was prepared. She started her announcement a millisecond before Troy started his. When he started to speak over her, she continued her announcement projecting as much as she could:

"Ladies and gentlemen, we are about to begin boarding flight 1300 here at gate B17A.1 with service to San Mira Vista Mar, California. Please take a moment to locate the group number on your boarding pass. Here at Intermittent Airlines, we board the rich first, followed by the slightly less rich, the disabled, and families traveling with small children."

At the adjacent gate, Troy continued the standard announcement, glaring at her from behind his com unit, speaking as loudly as he possibly could in an attempt to drown her out:

"If you are in group two, excellent work! You had your finger hovering above the check-in button exactly twenty-four hours ahead of time! If you are in group three, you were tardy, and if you are in groups four or five, we actually don't have room for you on this flight. Please take out your anger at the nearest customer service station!"

Both ended their announcements by asking passengers in group one to line up. The passengers knew something had been announced and figured it was probably close to boarding time. So, they all stood up and gathered in a confused mass in front of their respective boarding doors.

The passengers *did* understand when boarding began, not because of anything the gate agents said, but because the agents motioned to the closest person to come forward. The people behind followed in a massive stampede.

Both Janice and Troy were too busy glaring at each other to notice that their wheelchair passengers were being trampled. In the end, everyone found their seats, and Intermittent Airlines only had a few lawsuits to settle.

That first day planted a deep and raging rivalry between the two gate agents. Their hatred was so strong that they started purposefully making announcements over each other even when they did not have flights departing at the same time.

Troy would start a boarding announcement, and Janice would jump in and gleefully say:

"Thank you for choosing Intermittent Airlines! We know you have many choices when you fly, and that you chose us because we were the cheapest option!"

Troy would counter, saying: *"Wanted to give those of you in the boarding area a little update! The flight here at gate B18A.2 has been delayed due to bird interference. This flight is now departing at 10:00 p.m. out of gate G67C.1. Start walking, you've got plenty of time!"*

As you can imagine, this rivalry led to chaotic boarding and angry passengers. However, Janice and Troy were never fired or separated. You see, no one could remember if they were employees of Intermittent Airlines, Mackerel Valley International Airport, or the Federal Government. They also couldn't remember whose job it was to find out.

Their peers all assumed this would continue indefinitely. The poor customer service agents despaired, thinking the stream of enraged customers would never end. Fortunately for them, it did end. Here is how it came about.

About three hundred passengers were waiting across the adjacent gate areas that day. A few had pets in crates, and one little old woman had an emotional support animal allowed on a leash. It was an evening flight, and a connection for most of the passengers. They were tired and cranky.

Janice started to announce boarding:

"Good evening, ladies and gentlemen–" she began.

"To those of you traveling with us to San Mira Vista Mar California, the weather is sunny, seventy-two degrees with a strong chance of smog and aggressive drivers!" Troy interrupted.

Janice spoke louder, ***"As a reminder, this is a completely full flight! So, if you are a woman, please scrunch up as tight as possible to avoid accidentally brushing the moist man flesh seeping over your armrest!"***

The rivalry grew until the announcements were not only garbled beyond recognition, but piercing.

The passengers started yelling and swarming the gate podium, trying to snatch the com units away, but Janice and Troy clung on and kept speaking, desperate to win the conflict.

As this unfolded, the little old woman in the gate area started rocking in her seat, mumbling to herself, and stroking the fur of her feline companion. She was already so afraid of flying, and all the commotion was making her heart race.

"Oh dear, oh dear, I'm so dreadfully frightened, Max," she kept mumbling while stroking his fur harder and harder.

Max was a good emotional support animal and sensed her distress. He decided he would put an end to the noise at once. In one great bound, he tore his leash out of the woman's hand and charged through the crowd. People dove aside as he sprang past. He gobbled up Troy first and then turned on the petrified Janice.

You see, Max was a lion. You are probably wondering how a lion was allowed through airport security. Normally, they aren't, and a security agent did question it. However, his manager reminded him that Max was wearing an orange vest and therefore had to be allowed through.

When the lion had finished his meal, some of the passengers returned to their seats while others went to customer service to demand replacement agents so they could continue with boarding.

The little old woman, however, gently stroked Max's fur and said in a tiny voice, "You're such a dear, Max. You always do know how to help me calm down!"

I am happy to say that the Mackerel Valley International Airport did eventually hire a cheerful employee. His name was Elmer, and he was a security dog. Each day, he would happily patrol the security lines, his tail wagging, sniffing travelers, and saying in doggish: "I will find the drugs, master! And the explosives too! I do promise I will! I will find all the illegal things! I am so excited to find the illegal things!"

Elmer loved his job, and he never had a bad day.

3

Amala Fights for Animal Rights

When Amala was telling the tragic story of Troy and Janice, she made a point to pause as the crowd swarmed the podium but before Max the lion put an end to the affair.

"I apologize, Minister," she yawned. "But I really should be going to bed. I have to get up very early tomorrow if I am to be thrown to the beavers."

Champagne looked confused. "But who won?"

"It's complicated," Amala replied. "But it's 9:30 now, and I don't have time to finish the story."

"I still have half a beer though," the prime minister continued.

"It occurs to me," Amala started. "That you've been throwing people to the beavers for at least two weeks now."

"And?" Champagne shrugged.

"It must be a lot of work for them—gnawing on people every day."

"I suppose," Champagne continued.

"If you postpone my mauling by one day, then the beavers will get a break. I can sleep in tomorrow and finish the rest of the story tonight."

Champagne thought. "Yeah, but I don't want your president to think I am going soft, you know?"

"Soft?" Amala gasped. "The Canadian prime minister? Never! Tell the president that you are trying to avoid an animal rights violation."

Champagne was tilting his head back and forth undecidedly.

"Do you think *she* cares about beaver's rights?" Amala pressed. "No! She'd work those beavers to death! Aren't you better than that?"

Champagne bit his lip thoughtfully.

"Well?" Amala demanded.

Stuart pounded a fist on the reception desk and pointed a threatening finger at the prime minister. "Let her finish!" he growled.

Champagne agreed, and so, Amala was able to finish recounting the tale.

The following evening, the prime minister returned to check on his prisoners. Amala was just switching off the 1995 hiking safety video when he walked in.

"Hi, prime minister!" she said.

"How's it goin'?" he replied.

"Great! You're just in time for my next story!"

"Oh, you're going to tell another one?" he asked.

"Sure, it's only 7:15," she shrugged. "I've got tons of time, and we are now all well versed in hiking safety, so what else are we going to do?"

"Well, okay, as long as it isn't too long," he agreed. He took a seat on a rustic pickle barrel, and Amala began.

4

Scott the CEO

cott Allen finally achieved his lifelong dream. The company he founded was about to go public. After a long career full of struggle and failure, success came in the form of a little finger protector for people who use touch screens.

A typical review from online retail sites looked like this:

Five stars: "The skin on my index finger was almost completely worn through from using touch screens all day until I found this handy thing! What a life saver!"

The company was called Tap Pro Inc. (TP for short) and in thirteen years they went from a one-man operation with a single finger protector model to a multinational organization with a dozen products for every person in every imaginable scenario.

Scott invented the product by cutting the finger off one of his gloves. As Scott hired more engineers, the product became more practical. The newer models resembled a contact lens that stuck on the fingertip. They were sleek. They were sexy. All the cool kids had one.

It was 12:00 a.m. the day before the initial public offering. After a long evening of celebrating with his colleagues, Scott returned to his office. His plan was simply to collect his briefcase and head home, but he was so intoxicated with his success (and also with alcohol), that he decided to flop into his chair and scroll through the product reviews one more time.

He pulled out his phone and drank in the words of his admiring public. To think he came from nothing and was now a millionaire. It was everything he ever wanted. He sighed. He was a month short of sixty. His father died at… he tried to think… seventy-three?

He endured a lifetime of failure for what? So he could enjoy thirteen years of success?

"Oh, how I wish I could endure as long as this great company of mine!" he bemoaned.

"Who are you talking to?" came a voice.

Scott startled. He hadn't realized he was speaking aloud. He looked wildly around the room before spotting her. She was standing directly in front of him.

She was wearing a suit with a knee length pencil skirt and heels so high they might as well have been stilts. She had a short power cut and modern glasses with thick blue frames. Her gaze was fixed on her phone.

Her appearance was flawless. There wasn't a crease on her blazer, or a stray hair on her head. It was almost like she had her clothes dry cleaned onto herself.

"Who are you?" he asked, bewildered.

"I am Eda the business fairy," she replied, without looking up from her phone. "Didn't you just make a wish?"

Scott squinted at her. "If you are a fairy, then why don't you have any wings?"

"Fairies don't actually have wings, Mr. Allen. Humans just draw us that way because…" She looked up, thinking for a moment. "I honestly have no idea why."

Scott scrutinized her a moment more. "Okay," he said. "If you are who you say you are, prove it! Do some magic."

"How about I answer all your password security questions?" she suggested.

"Alright. Go on! Go on!"

"Your mother's maiden name is Smith, you went to Mackerel Valley High School, and your first pet's name was Fluffy1234. (Well, the numbers aren't actually part of the name. You just added them to make the answer harder to guess.)"

Scott's bloodshot eyes widened. He was amazed.

"So you really are a fairy!" he exclaimed.

Technology was not Scott's strong suit, and he could never find the time to take the quarterly cyber security training. So, while Eda was a real fairy, she wasn't answering Scott's password questions by magic. She was looking at his Wikipedia page. (She'd guessed about the numbers at the end of Fluffy's name.)

Scott was too excited to notice. "This must be some kind of a fairy tale, or, or maybe a fable!" He was ecstatic but collected himself enough to explain: "A fable is a short story with a mor–"

"Thank you, Mr. Allen," she answered. "I am a fairy. I know what a fable is."

"If this is a fairy tale, then I must be the hero!"

"Hmmm…" thought Eda with a little shrug. "*Protagonist*, sure."

"And I can wish for anything?"

"Well, anything business related," she replied. "I'll have to refer you to another fairy for other requests. And you said something about wanting to endure like your company or whatever, so do you want it or not?"

"More than anything!" Scott answered.

"Cool, I've got a meeting in five so let me just…" she tapped her phone a couple of times and flipped it around revealing some text and a signature line. "Check the box that says you've read and agreed to all the terms and conditions, then sign with your finger."

Scott checked the box. He hadn't read all the terms and conditions of course, but since no one ever does, he didn't worry. He signed.

The fairy took her phone back and raised an eyebrow. His signature was illegible even when he used a ballpoint pen. A touch screen made it horrifying.

She shrugged and pocketed her phone. "We're all set, Mr. Allen. Your health is now directly intertwined with that of Tap Pro Inc. When TP is doing well, so will you. If TP is doing poorly, you will also."

"Wait," Scott said. "…intertwined with TP? That's not what I wished for!"

"It states very clearly in the terms and–"

"Right, right, of course!" he interjected. "Yes, clearly."

He wasn't worried. After all, TP was thriving. What could possibly go wrong?

Eda gave him a firm handshake. "Get some sleep, Mr. Allen," she said. "You've got a bell to ring tomorrow."

Scott pulled his car keys out of his pocket as Eda turned to leave.

"You're not driving, are you?" she asked.

"I'm fine," he insisted. "Have you seen my phone?"

"You're holding it, Mr. Allen," she answered, pulling out her own.

"Would you look at that!" he observed with a laugh and a shake of his head.

Eda tapped on her phone a couple of times. "Go down to the lobby, Mr. Allen. In a few moments, a magical, driverless car will arrive to take you home."

Once again, Scott was amazed.

For the next year, Scott felt better than ever before. He woke without aches and pains, ran without losing his breath, and even resumed playing sports when he had the time.

His friends and family noticed he looked better but couldn't determine what was different.

Stocks were rising, reviews were gushing, business was booming, and the company grew. Every employee from the vice president of accounting to the cubical cleaner's intern was going above and beyond because they felt like they were part of something great.

Then one day, as Scott sat in a conference watching one of his executives present. He sneezed.

The sensation shocked him. You might think it strange that a sneeze would shock anyone, but Scott had gone a full year without sneezing once.

"…So as you can see," the exec droned, pointing to a line chart. "This black line is going up and this redline is going down. This means my organization is doing useful things. Can we have more money?"

Scott was still staring into his hand. He sniffled. "Um… sorry, can you say that last part again?"

Unfortunately, things only got worse for Scott. Over the next few weeks, he was plagued by sniffles and sneezes of all kinds. He found himself carrying dozens of tissue packets with him everywhere and entering panics when he ran out. A colleague suggested it was spring allergies. But Scott didn't believe this because he never had allergies and it wasn't spring.

He remembered his contract with Eda but felt certain that couldn't be causing the problems. After all, if TP was doing well, he should be also.

Then his personal assistant politely suggested that perhaps he was under stress and should take a vacation. Scott was delighted with this diagnosis and in short order found himself lying on a beach in Belize. He was reading a book he purchased at the airport newsstand. It was titled: *Tried and True: Old School Tactics for Driving Your Modern Business.*

With his ball cap, Hawaiian shirt, khaki shorts, and sandals over white socks, he was an abomination in the eyes of fashion. The salt air and warm sand didn't make him feel any less sneezy, but at least he was getting some R&R.

"Enjoying yourself, Mr. Allen?" came a familiar voice.

Scott sat bolt upright. Strolling across the sand was Eda.

Scott would have been alarmed by her sudden appearance had he not been so distracted by her feet. She was wearing the very same pair of heels as the day they met, but they did not sink into the sand as she crossed the beach.

"You shouldn't walk on sand in shoes like that," Scott observed. "Heels are the leading cause of foot injuries in women."

Eda smiled sweetly. "Thank you, Mr. Allen. I really don't know how I've survived all these thousands of years without you around to tell me these things."

Scott returned her smile; glad she appreciated his advice.

"But I didn't come here to talk about my shoes," she continued. "I came to check in on you. Heard you weren't feeling so well."

"I'm fine," Scott sneezed.

"Oh?"

"Of course," he replied. "TP's never been better and neither have I. Besides, given our success, if something were wrong with me, you'd be in violation of your contract."

"The contract is perfect, and the magic is working perfectly," Eda replied. "If you weren't feeling well, it would only be because something is wrong with your company."

"Like what?" Scott asked. "I mean, hypothetically, if something were wrong with me?"

"This is a fairy tale, Mr. Allen," Eda replied. "And I am a fairy. If you've read any fairy tales, you should know I can't give you a straight answer about anything."

"Why not?" Scott pressed.

She answered him directly: "Because then you wouldn't learn anything. Also, the story would be too short."

Scott was growing impatient. "If something were wrong with me, what would you do?"

"I would—I will give you something that will help you learn the answer for yourself. Go back to work, Mr. Allen and you'll understand."

She tossed him a packet of tissues and was gone before Scott could reply. She seemed to disappear into thin air.

Perhaps she had. She was a fairy after all, but more likely, she ran away really quickly while he blinked. I suppose we'll never know for sure.

No one recognized Scott when he returned to work. It could have been that he had traded in his usual grey suit for a plaid button up and jeans, but most likely, it was the false mustache.

He had a brilliant plan. He figured the best way to learn what was really amiss at TP, was to lose his CEO status. He felt certain his employees were more likely to be honest with Gary from facilities than with Scott the CEO. Besides, being from facilities meant he could wander all around the campus and no one would suspect anything. If anyone asked, he was doing a mandatory lightbulb inspection.

Scott was up on a ladder examining his first bulb, when he discovered Eda's gift. He was on a floor with open cubes. There were thirty or so conversations taking place across the room. Scott found that regardless of where the conversations took place, he could focus in and hear any of them.

He heard two salesmen standing by the printer, lamenting the outcome of last night's game. He heard a woman from marketing on the opposite side of the room asking a peer if a particular shade of violet was in compliance with brand standards. He heard two IT support agents coming out of the elevator joking about how TP actually stood for toilet paper.

He scowled. It took just over a million dollars and a small army of branding experts to come up with the initialism TP. Had they no respect?

It occurred to Scott that listening to conversations this way might not be legal. He'd ask Eda to un-enchant him next time he saw her, but in the meantime, he would just have to deal with it.

Scott moved on to inspect his next lightbulb and passed a closed office door. He heard voices from the other side and listened carefully. Sure enough, his ability to focus worked even through doors. He shook his head at the idea that Eda would give him such an unethical gift, then listened to the conversation taking place.

"I can't do this if I have to go through Jason," a woman's voice said. "The man's an idiot. If he had to approve everything I did, I'd get nothing done!"

"I know," came a sympathetic reply. "Let me talk to him, maybe I'll buy him a drink."

"Great idea," answered the first voice. "Give him enough alcohol and he'll approve anything!"

Both voices laughed.

Scott moved on. While inspecting his next light bulb he heard a man and woman speaking by the coffee pot.

"Did you see the research department?" the woman asked.

"No," the man smiled.

"They have their cubes all decorated! It's amazing! Little bells made out of cups, paper chains, everything!"

The man laughed. "Wow, they really went all out, didn't they?"

"They sure did!" The woman replied. "Must be nice to have so much free time!"

The man responded with a smirk and an eye roll. "Come on, Maggie, you know research doesn't actually do anything at this company."

So it continued. In every hallway, in every lunchroom, everywhere all over the company Scott heard people speak similarly. Each team thought they were the hardest working, the smartest, and the only ones who actually cared about success. The entire campus was infected with toxic murmurs.

A light bulb went on over Scott's head (actually it was more of a fluorescent tube), and just at the same moment, he had an idea.

About a week later, all TP employees gathered for a companywide meeting. Scott ensured there would be a massive turnout by providing free donuts. He watched as they filed into the largest conference room in the building in search of the pastries disguised as breakfast food.

The topic of the meeting was company culture. In his presentation, Scott talked about how other companies were promoting a healthy workplace environment. How research proved that such efforts were good for business. He showed stock photos of happy business professionals having picnics and playing golf. He firmly declared that gossip was not part of the company culture.

His employees watched with eyes as glazed as the donuts they were steadily consuming.

He concluded by announcing that he was going to hire a vice president of employee relations to enforce a positive and productive workplace environment.

When the presentation was over, he returned to his office feeling pleased with himself. He was so confident that his allergies would cease, that he took all his tissue boxes to the roof and threw them off—an action he was bound to regret.

Scott was angry. It had been several months since the company meeting. TP's profits continued to grow, they had launched a new product successfully, and yet he was continually feeling weak and nauseous.

He hoped that Eda would turn up and set things right. But when weeks passed and she did not, he decided to make an appointment with his doctor.

Doctor Randy Webb was an enthusiastic man whose caffeine addiction was evidenced by his wide eyes, jittering hands, and seldom ceasing chatter. He listened to Scott describe his symptoms, then said with a bright smile: "Sounds like pregnancy! But that can't be since you're a man! It's probably just cancer."

He waited for Scott to laugh.

Scott did not laugh.

"So… anyway," Dr. Webb continued. "We'll run some tests. If you don't hear from me, everything's fine."

"And if I hear from you?" Scott asked.

Webb's expression became dark. "Pray."

The phone rang in Scott's office early the next morning.

"Hello Scott, how are you doing today?" came Dr. Webb's chipper voice.

Scott wasn't sure, so he lied in the customary fashion: "Fine."

"Ah good," Webb continued. "So, the test results came back and well… your cells are multiplying in all kinds of ways that they shouldn't…"

"What are you saying?" Scott demanded.

"Remember how yesterday I made that joke about you having cancer? Well, you actually do!" The doctor laughed. "Now isn't that something?"

Scott hung up the phone. Before he had a chance to reflect on his woeful situation, the door to his office opened.

In walked Eda, her gaze glued to her phone. Somehow, she navigated into the room and gracefully around all the ill-placed furniture without taking her eyes off the screen.

"You!" Scott cried, leaping from his chair with such force it went spinning across the room.

"Hello, Mr. Allen," she returned.

"Where have you been?" he snapped. "Did you know this would happen?"

"Know what would happen?" she replied.

"That I'd get cancer!"

"Cancer," she mumbled. "Makes sense it would manifest itself that way, given the duplication of cells and all."

"You did this to me, didn't you?"

"I did nothing," Eda replied. "You always knew this was a possibility, Scott. It stated very clearly in the terms and–"

"How can I have cancer when the company is doing so well?" he demanded.

She held up a finger. "One moment…" She tapped at her smartphone.

"What are you doing?" he snapped.

"Selling some stock," she answered.

"If that's TP stock I'll have you arrested for insider trading," he grumbled.

"It's only insider trading if I possess material non-public information."

"Ah! But you do!" Scott replied "You see, material means that a reasonable investor would care about it—"

"Thank you, Mr. Allen, I know what material means," Eda explained. "And you expect any reasonable investor to believe that you entered into a magical contract with a business fairy?"

Scott frowned. "I suppose not… but I have cancer! Very bad, probably going to die! There, now you know something a reasonable investor would care about! Ha!"

"Maybe… There could be any number of outcomes," Eda thought. "I probably should consult with Law Fairy[1] first."

She pocketed her phone.

Scott laughed triumphantly.

"But I did not come here for legal advice, Scott." She took a seat. "Let's see if we can find a way to change your outcome."

Scott fetched his chair and slumped down in it.

---

1   Law Fairy asked me to remind you that this is a fictional short story designed for entertainment purposes only. Nothing written here should be construed as legal advice. The author of this short story does not make recommendations about whether or not to trade in shares for any company. Further, the laws governing trading in Para Sympan may not directly align to the laws in your universe. If you have questions about the legality of making a trade, please consult an expert from your own world. Further, it should be noted that reading this short story may cause cancer in the State of California. If you aren't in California, don't worry about it.

"Remember the vice president of employee relations you hired? Debra?"

"Of course, she's the very reason I shouldn't be in this situation," he grumbled.

"On the contrary, Mr. Allen," Eda replied. "I'm afraid Debra is the reason, well, one of many."

"Get to the point," Scott demanded. "And no more of this cryptic fairy nonsense, I want a straight answer."

"I'll humor you," Eda agreed. "You see, Debra started at TP under the assumption that your employee relations problems were due to the destructive policies put in place by Alley's department."

Alley's department was HR.

"What destructive policies?" Scott asked.

"There are none," Eda answered. "But there were destructive policies at many of Debra's past organizations. Thus, her assumption."

"Why did she assume? Why not just talk to Alley?"

"Well, she discussed it with Jerry," Eda explained.

"But Jerry's in finance." Scott sputtered.

"Yes, but you see, Jerry and Debra are already acquainted. They used to meet up every year at Phoney Con before they came to work for TP. So naturally Debra mentioned her concerns to Jerry, while they were having lunch on Tuesday. Now, Jerry cautioned Debra not to speak to Alley–"

"Wait, why not?"

"Because," Eda explained. "How did Jerry put it… 'Alley is a witch.' Jerry then proceeded to tell Debra all about his horrible experiences working with Alley."

"But gossip is not part of our company culture!" Scott interjected.

"Now, now, Mr. Allen," Eda replied, raising a finger. "They are executives. They know that. Jerry wasn't gossiping, he was just *venting*. After all it isn't good to keep your frustrations bottled up."

Scott made no reply as he tried to work out what Eda was saying. She did not wait for him to comprehend, just pressed on.

"Debra decided to handle TP's gossip problem by creating the Employee Conflict Resolution Team to pinpoint where tension existed between departments and work to resolve it."

"I don't see what's wrong with that," Scott observed.

"Nothing at all," Eda continued. "Except, had Debra talked to Alley, she'd have found that Alley already has a team doing just that—The Cross Departmental Collaboration Team.

"Now the Cross Departmental Collaboration Team heard about the Employee Conflict Resolution Team and were distressed. Instead of trying to unify their efforts, the teams began to compete for resources. So, the Employee Conflict Resolution Team refused to work with the Cross Departmental Collaboration Team. In the end, TP had two separate teams doing exactly the same work."

"So, we just need to merge both teams or get rid of one of them," Scott reasoned.

"I wish it was that simple," Eda replied. "But you'll find similar conflict blossoming all over the company. For example, you probably noticed the tension between John from research and Jamie from sales."

Scott hadn't, but he was beginning to think there was a lot he didn't notice.

"John refuses to work with Jamie because Alley told him about a time when Jamie purposefully deprioritized her employee survey because she'd delivered bad news about his approval ratings as a vice president. And it gets worse, Sam from—"

"Stop! Stop! Stop!" Scott demanded. "I get the picture! No one is talking to anyone else; teams are duplicating, trust is crumbling…" He sat for a moment, finger on his chin, thinking.

"What if we restructure the entire organization?" Scott suggested. "We'll start by making Debra head of HR."

"Wait a moment," Eda said. "Debra's been nothing but toxic since you brought her in, why would you give her the entire HR department?"

"Because the only other option is to leave Alley in charge of HR and have Debra report to her. Then again," he thought. "I could move Alley out of HR altogether and have her run something else."

"Or you could fire Debra," Eda suggested.

"Fire Debra!" Scott exclaimed. "Just like that?"

"Well, no, not 'just like that', give her a warning first and time to improve, then fire her if she doesn't."

"I can't fire Debra!" Scott insisted.

"Why not? You've fired employees for similar destructive behavior, haven't you?"

"Maybe," Scott replied. "But not at the executive level. You can't fire an executive for gossiping!"

"Why–" Eda began, but Scott cut her off talking almost as much to himself as to her.

"If you fire an executive for something that trivial, investors will start thinking you are in some kind of trouble!"

"But you are–"

Scott cut Eda off again. "Not to mention the fact that Jerry would resent me if I fired her. The whole staff would! As bosses go, I am pretty well liked and this would ruin my image."

"You talk like you've never fired anyone," Eda observed.

"Of course not!" Scott replied. "I've never made a bad hire!"

Eda responded with stunned silence. Then finally said: "Don't you have thirty years experience?"

"Almost forty," Scott proudly stated.

"How did you get to be CEO?"

Scott responded by falling into his elevator pitch: "It began when I cut the finger off one of my gloves! Little did I know that this invention would revolutionize the smartphone accessories industry!"

"Right, you invented the product," Eda said. She thought for a moment. "Have you ever considered taking a more product focused role?"

"Change my role?" Scott was alarmed. "You mean, step down from being CEO?"

Eda nodded. "Sure, then you could actually create something. You like inventing things, and you must be good at it because consumers love your products."

Scott was turning scarlet. The only thing he heard was: "Step down, Scott", "You're too old, Scott.", and "You're incompetent, Scott."

Eda hadn't said any of these things but that didn't stop them from festering in Scott's mind.

"I created this company!" Scott cried. "I caused its growth! It went public because of me! And you want me to step down?"

Eda was confused. "I don't want anything," she explained. "What happens to TP doesn't affect me in the slightest. I am just making a suggestion."

"I've worked my whole life for this! And I am not going to surrender this company to anyone! Unlike you, I can't just make things happen with a snap of my fingers! I created this company and there's no one in the world more qualified to run it."

He looked as if he was going to jump across his desk and strangle her. Eda watched his outburst with a slightly bored expression then glanced down at her phone for the time.

When he finished, she said simply: "What you do is entirely up to you."

She disappeared.

Scott decided to restructure the entire company. After this took place, he got a call from Dr. Webb recommending they try a controversial new treatment.

"In layman's terms," Dr. Webb explained. "We are going to remove the tumors and then implant them elsewhere in your body."

"That's insanity!" Scott exclaimed. "Has that ever worked before?"

"No," Dr. Webb replied. "But we are absolutely confident it will work for you!"

The doctor did sound confident, and Scott was desperate, so he submitted to the treatment. Unfortunately, Scott's health only deteriorated further. In fact, as TP's employees shared their theories about what was behind the restructure, the cancer spread at an alarming rate.

Despite his failing health, Scott continued coming to work. His colleagues kept suggesting he go on leave, but the more they pressed him the more he insisted on staying. "I'll quit when I'm dead!" he would say. TP was his and he'd surrender it to no one.

The gossip at TP soon turned to resentment and backstabbing. In fact, TP's employees were so busy trying to take each other down, that they failed to notice a competitor was stealing away their business.

Scott was declared dead the very moment TP declared bankruptcy. For weeks afterward, employees, consumers, and investors wondered if this was a coincidence or if the combined forces of Scott's failing health and failing business drove him to end his life early. Some even went so far as to say Scott was murdered by competitors.

Scott's autopsy showed that he was actually killed by a vicious autoimmune disease. This left Dr. Webb scratching his head and rambling to his peers: "It's marvelous! Amazing! I've never seen anything like it! Here the man is already dying of cancer but in the end, it's his own body that kills him! I've never seen a disease like this! It's my new favorite! Can I name it?"

Although Scott's body was in horrible condition, the hospital decided donating his organs was an excellent idea. In the very moment they were being harvested, TP's former employees were out looking for work with other organizations.

And while all this was unfolding, Eda was on the deck of her new yacht, sipping margaritas and grumbling about how humans never really learn anything.

Maybe Scott didn't learn his lesson, but that doesn't mean you can't learn from this fable.

The moral of the story is always read the terms and conditions.

Actually, that's not the moral. You're smart, you figure it out.

5

Amala Avoids Desludging the Coffee Pot

"This one's easy," Champagne said as Amala finished. "The actual moral is that fairies shouldn't invest in the stock market."

"Yeah, it's pretty obvious if you were paying attention. Now, *Lethal Love*, there's a story—" Amala glanced at the clock. "Oh, never mind."

"What about what?" Champagne pressed.

"It's an unrelated story but I don't have time to tell it now. I promised Stuart I would desludge the coffee pot before bed and I am going to be thrown to the beavers in the morning."

"Right," Champagne answered. "But honestly, is it even possible to desludge that coffee pot?"

"It's been ten years since my last attempt," Stuart shrugged. "Pro'ly need a drill."

"Then I'd better get started!" Amala exclaimed.

"Someone else can do it," Champagne suggested gesturing to the small crowd of prisoners milling around the lobby.

"No can do," Stuart replied. "I've already given the others jobs."

"What other jobs?" the prime minister asked.

Stuart started pointing at people. "Joe's removing the mystery stains from the hall carpet, Britney is immobilizing the springs in the vending machine, and Steve is looking for the piece from the lobby puzzle that's been missing for thirteen years. Oh, and Martin is refilling those little shampoo bottles. Do you know how long it takes to refill those shampoo bottles?"

"Aren't most weekends two days?" Amala pointed out.

"Sure, but why—"

"So those beavers should have two days off, right?"

"Four days!" Stuart interjected. They've been working for two weeks straight. We owe 'em."

"I guess," Champagne shrugged.

Everyone cheered and while they all went about their unsavory tasks, Amala entertained them with a heartbreaking tale of young love and loss.

6

Lethal Love

James had everything a young man could want, well, almost everything. He had a full scholarship to Rouvin University where he was a straight A student. He had a paid internship at Tap Pro Inc. and was building out a plan for his own business. He had a mother and father who loved him and a sweet grandmother he visited every other weekend.

Yet, even with all this, he felt himself incomplete. You see James was waiting to meet *the one*. The girl he couldn't stop thinking about, the girl he would do anything for, the girl who would make his life full and rich.

Julie was a biology major. She worked as a barista at the campus coffee shop and spent all her free time volunteering at a local wildlife rehabilitation center. She found her volunteer work most fulfilling and hoped she could eventually get a full-time job working with animals.

There was only one thing missing from her life and that was Mr. Right.

hen one fateful day it happened. James entered the campus coffee shop and ordered a sixteen-ounce cup filled with as many espresso shots as would fit. He had a midterm early the next morning and was preparing for a long afternoon of study.

He was standing next to the pickup counter scrolling through the study guide on his phone, when a beautiful voice rang out:

"James!"

He looked up and saw her peeking out from behind the towering espresso machine. He noticed the curls of her auburn hair sticking out from under her green uniform cap. Her hazel eyes, the gentle curve of her face, she was like an angel.

Julie noticed him too, his scruffy black hair, his untucked button-up and his deep brown eyes that seemed to swallow her soul.

In that moment, they both had the same thought: this must be *the one*!

James skipped all the way back to his apartment. He knew it was crazy, he knew it was reckless, but he also knew that Julie was *the one*. The person who would make him complete. So, he took the chance, he asked her to dinner, and she accepted. It was like the universe was smiling down on him and everything was falling into place.

He moved his hand upward in a coffee drinking motion, only to realize he didn't have his drink. He was so entranced with Julie, that he left his coffee sitting on the pickup counter. Normally, such a revelation would have led to panic, but not today. How could he worry about a little caffeine deprivation when he had finally found *the one?*

He spent the whole afternoon preparing for the date (researching to find the best dining options, buying flowers, ironing his suit again and again.) He wanted everything to be perfect. After all, he knew this girl was his other half. The person who would complete him.

ulie's heart was pounding. Butterflies fluttered in her chest. She lost her concentration. She forgot to put espresso in an old professor's drink and added it to a small child's chocolate milk instead. She wrote the wrong name on almost every cup, even misspelling the name Ed.

Her fingers were unsteady, her mind was elsewhere. She hardly noticed the mob of angry customers swarming the pickup counter yelling obscenities.

A boy had asked her on a date—a real, live boy! She had never been sure of anything in her life until now. He was *the one*, her missing piece!

When her concerned manager asked her if she wanted to leave early, Julie fled the building. There was so much to do: shower, second shower, hair, make-up, call all her girlfriends for advice… She had no idea how she would do everything in time!

When James came to pick her up that evening, they were both so overwhelmed they could hardly speak. So they didn't. They just sort of giggled as they skipped hand in hand to the restaurant.

Unfortunately, neither of them realized they were skipping down the path to their own demise.

he next few weeks were blissful for the new couple. They spent hours gazing into each other's eyes, whispering sweet nothings, and holding hands while spinning slowly through wheat fields.

Normally, James would have been horrified to learn that he failed a midterm (after all he never failed anything in his life), but he just didn't care. What was one midterm to a man in love?

Julie's grades were also falling. She couldn't focus on her books and daydreamed through class. She even freed all the mice from the lab once with the gentle words: "How can I vivisect you, little friends? I'm in love!"

The mice then joined her in a musical number about her newfound feelings. It came to an abrupt end when her horrified professor entered.

James' advisor reminded him that he needed to keep his grades up or he'd lose his scholarship. James noted this, then fled the meeting as soon as he was dismissed, eager to be with Julie.

This continued for weeks. Julie stopped volunteering at the animal rehab so she could spend more time staring at the clouds with James. After several missed shifts, the rehab asked her not to come back. She was disappointed at first, but then figured it didn't matter as long as she had her other half.

Finally, James' advisor regretfully informed him that he'd lost his scholarship. James was horrified and spent the next several classroom hours wondering what happened. He ignored all the calls from his parents, since he did not want to speak with them until he had a plan. He needed to find time to resume his studies and bring his grades back up but did not want to use any of the precious time he had with Julie.

He decided he'd skip the visit to his grandmother's, at least for a couple of weeks until he was able to get his scholarship back. This led to more calls from his parents which he ignored.

Julie finally lost her job at the cafe and ran tearfully into the arms of James. Together they bemoaned the cruelty of the universe.

"Not to worry, my darling," James reassured. "I still have my job with TP Inc. when I graduate, we can get married, I'll support us both!"

Julie was overwhelmed with joy. She gave up all thoughts of being a biologist and spent every moment dreaming of being the perfect wife. She didn't need her dreams; James would complete her!

James was shocked the day TP declared bankruptcy. He was so depressed, he didn't even bother to collect his box of cubical ornaments and sticky notes. He'd no scholarship, no job, angry parents, and was months behind on his business plan. But he still had Julie, what more did he need to be complete?

Then it came to him. Julie was the only thing in the world that mattered anymore, and he was going to show her that. He was going to do something crazy, something reckless, something illegal, something his parents would never approve of, and all for Julie!

He was going to spray paint her name on the underside of the Mackerel Valley River Bridge.

It was an old, open spandrel bridge made up of three arches, each hopping over a different obstacle. The first obstacle was the Mackerel Valley Expressway, the central arch spanned Mackerel Valley River itself, and the third spanned the cleverly named River Road North West.

It was a beautiful piece of historic masonry and James felt the only thing that could make it more lovely was the name of his beloved in radiation green. He planned to do it right in the center of the arch over the expressway where it would be most visible.

He arrived in the middle of the afternoon with a backpack full of paint cans. If you think vandalizing such a public place in broad daylight is a bad idea, you are absolutely right. However, James was new to being a rebel and frankly, he didn't care if all the world saw him immortalizing that heavenly name.

The area was busy, cars zipped up and down the expressway and a group of workmen cleared away the brush from the roadside. James strolled past the workers, trying to act casual while keeping out of sight behind their heavy machinery. He ducked past a tractor, a cherry picker, and then finally began his climb up the bridge from the shadow of a woodchipper that was parked beneath.

The workmen were so engrossed in the chopping of trees and clearing of weeds, they didn't notice James as he edged around the spandrel columns toward the center of the first arch.

But someone else did.

"James?" cried a familiar voice.

James looked up to see the face of his other half staring down at him from over the railing.

"James, no!" cried Julie. "You still have me, remember? And plenty of companies make pointless smartphone accessories, you'll find another job! I promise!"

James was confused until he saw other faces peering over the railing, some with expressions of mild curiosity, others wide-eyed with horror. It was only then that James realized they all thought he was going to jump.

James laughed. It was a reckless laugh that could only come from a man in love. "Oh Julie, I could never leave you! I've climbed this bridge for you!"

"But why?" she called.

"Because love is a crazy thing—a wild, uncontrollable thing! It should be proclaimed from the mountaintops, but since there are no mountains here, I've chosen the side of this bridge. I am going to paint your name here on top of the world!"

A few of the bystanders awed, but most just grumbled and went about their business.

Julie pressed her hand to her heart. "Oh James," she called. "My name would be incomplete without yours!" She climbed over the railing and began working her way down to him. She ignored the garbled warnings coming from the police bullhorns at the top of the bridge and the swearing of the workers below.

Finally, she joined him at his perch. Then, clinging to the masonry, they each spray painted the other's name in such a way as to make a seasoned graffiti artist smack his face to his palm. Then, hand in hand, they began inching back around the columns toward the base of the bridge and safety.

When they made it to the last column, Julie gazed into James' eyes.

"You complete me," she whispered.

"And you me," James returned.

He leaned in to kiss her.

But I am afraid this story doesn't end with a kiss. You see as they reached for each other, James lost his footing and tumbled off the bridge. Instinctively, his grip tightened on Julie's hand and she too slipped off her perch.

Together they fell straight into the open funnel of the woodchipper below.

And that is how James and Julie tore each other apart.

7

Amala the Misogynist

"Oh jeez, that was violent," Champagne observed.

"Well, sometimes fables have to be gruesome to effectively teach their morals. Speaking of which, did you ever figure out what the moral of that story is?"

"I mean, parking a woodchipper under a bridge probably violates a dozen safety regulations."

"Bingo!" Amala replied. "You're a smart man, prime minister!"

"F'ing Socrates," Stewart grumbled. He didn't say "f'ing", but he was taking a swig of beer as he spoke, and so that's what everyone heard.

"More like Rouvin," Amala corrected.

"Oh, um, yer actually not allowed to talk about Rouvin here," Champagne explained.

"What do you mean?" Amala asked. "He's the greatest philosopher in history."

"Yeah, but he said an offensive thing," Champagne explained. "And Canada is a safe space."

"Funny, I don't feel very safe here," Amala noticed.

"Well, it for sure isn't safe for misogynists like you," Champagne returned.

"How am I a misogynist?"

"You mentioned the name of an old dead guy with backwards ideas."

"I mean some of his ideas were backward, but a lot of what he said was quite progressive for his time."

"He literally said that women are incapable of reason," Champagne insisted.

"Sure he did," Amala answered. "It's incredible how some of the most intelligent people in history can come to such foolish conclusions."

"He couldn't have been that intelligent if he said women are incapable of reason," Champagne pressed.

"Oh, but he was, there's a whole story about him and how he was confused. And since we are giving the beavers four days off, I have time to tell it to you."

"There I draw the line!" Champagne exclaimed. Weeks without access to hockey was finally starting to wear on him. "I won't betray my voters by talking to a misogynist about a misogynist."

"The internet is down," Amala pointed out. "How are they ever going to know?"

Champagne glanced around the room at the small crowd of US citizens.

"No one here is a Canadian voter, either." Amala added. "I mean, except Stuart."

"And I didn't vote for you," Stuart growled.

Champagne furrowed his brow. "I'll be sitting here," he answered. "But I won't be listening."

8

Rouvin the Philosopher

The people of Helevina know very well that one's ability to reason is directly proportional to the length of one's beard. Now there was a man who lived in Helevina a very long time ago, whose beard was particularly long. His face was especially stern because he'd wrinkled his forehead with so much thinking. His name was Rouvin and he was a philosopher. But Rouvin wasn't just any philosopher, he was arguably the greatest philosopher in history.

He wrote about everything from the nature of thought, to the human soul, to God Himself. Though his teachings caused his students to gape, scribes to scribble furiously, and the kings of the world to seek his counsel, the only thing they brought to God was an amused little smile.

This is Rouvin's story, and I regret to say, it is not a happy one. It begins when he was just a young man. (Even in his youth he was bearded. In fact, historical evidence suggests he was born bearded.) He lived in a little village on the eastern side of Helevina that overlooked the sea. It was here that he first learned to wonder, and the delight he experienced in wondering was so sweet that once he began, he never voluntarily ceased.

Day in and day out he would watch the world, question it, contemplate it, test his conclusions, and finally put them on paper. He spent so much time doing this, he would have starved to death if it hadn't been for a young lady from the village. She would remind him to eat, remind him to sleep, and when she visited his home, she cleaned it thoroughly and scolded him for allowing it to fall into disarray. She was as practical as he was theoretical and as down to Earth as he was absent minded. Her name was Sophia, and Rouvin was very fond of her. As long as she was by his side, all his temporal needs were cared for and he was free to think.

She was fond of him also, for she could see that he had a brilliant mind and their conversations inspired and enriched her. Together they were happy…at first.

As time went on, Rouvin was consumed by his work more and more. He became so engrossed in his thoughts on the social nature of man that he stopped conversing with Sophia. Then, so busy penning his work on the nature of human affection that he forgot to offer her any. While he wrote seven hundred pages about the nature of human emotion, he failed to notice her growing frustration.

All this took place over the course of three years, and toward the end of the third year, Rouvin the philosopher began what is widely considered his greatest work. To this day, the work drives even the most stately academics to sobbing for its sheer splendor. He titled it: *On Marriage and the Nature of Love.*

On the very day that he was putting the final touches on this great work, Sophia decided to confront him. She was carrying a basket of his togas out to wash, when she noticed him sitting in his usual place scribbling furiously onto a scroll. She paused before him, silently reading his words.

She cleared her throat. Rouvin jumped, his pen flying from his hand. He looked up toward her bewildered.

"You have said that an actual thing is greater than the idea of a thing," Sophia began.

The philosopher shook off his confusion and smiled.

"Quite so!" he replied, both alarmed and delighted by her understanding.

"It follows then," she continued. "That actual marriage is greater than the idea of marriage."

Rouvin thought for a moment, then answered: "Why yes! That's exactly right. I'm so glad that you are beginning to understand these things, my dear!" With that, he began searching for his pen. Finding it, he turned his attention back to his writing.

After a few moments, he glanced up. She was still standing there, staring at him, her brow furrowed and her jaw tight.

"Was there something else you wanted?" he asked.

Her hand clenched the handle of the basket so that it almost snapped in two, but her expression did not change.

"I suppose actual clean laundry is also greater than the idea of clean laundry," she stated.

"I suppose so," he answered, raising an eyebrow. He wasn't sure why she was still on this subject.

"But since you seem content to live in the world of ideas…" she dumped the basket on his head and stormed out.

When she did not come home the following day, he went out into the village to look for her. His neighbors told him she had left by ship to seek her fortune in Athens.

Now Rouvin was arguably the most brilliant man that ever lived. And while he'd answered some of the greatest questions in the universe, he could not make sense of Sophia's behavior.

He spent many a long evening sitting alone among his scrolls, sipping wine, and contemplating this question. Indeed, he thought about it so much that his hair turned white, and his face became frozen in a scowl. At last, he finally came to a conclusion and penned his most infamous work. If you asked your philosophy professor about it, I guarantee he will deny its existence.

The work is titled: *On the Nature of Women*. In this work, Rouvin concludes that women are so enslaved by their emotions that they are completely incapable of reason.

Having satisfied himself with the idea that Sophia's behavior was a result of her feminine nature, he decided to move onto other questions. Further, he resolved never to interact with a woman again. Of course, this was easier said than done, due to the inconvenient fact that women made up half the human population. And it only became more difficult after that fateful day when Lysander the Conqueror attacked.

J f you ask a child what he wants to be when he grows up, he might say a doctor, a firefighter, or an engineer. When Lysander the Conqueror was a little boy, his mother asked him this very question. He answered: "I want to rule the world!" His mother laughed and patted him on the head. What she didn't realize is that one day he would actually do it.

Lysander valued three things above all else: books, conquering (obviously), and his darling war horse Calla. He would have married Calla if he could, but marrying horses was frowned upon in those days even for the ruler of the world.

The day Lysander invaded, Rouvin was so absorbed in thought, he failed to notice the attack on his village until one of the conqueror's warriors broke down the door. The man would have killed the terrified philosopher right then and there if Lysander himself hadn't intervened. You see, when the invader stormed in, one of Rouvin's scrolls came rolling out into the street. Lysander (being a lover of books and all) stopped killing people for a moment so he could read it. The work was called: *On Horses: Highest of Animals*.

The conqueror rushed to the house. Luckily for Rouvin, the invading soldier, blade raised for the kill, paused mid-blow. It was the kind of hesitation one has when one is about to kill the protagonist of an incomplete story. It gave Lysander just enough time to burst in shouting: "stop!"

Then catching his breath, he held the open scroll out toward Rouvin. "Did you write this?" he demanded.

The wide-eyed philosopher nodded.

"Wonderful!" the conqueror exclaimed. "You'll come back to the capital with me and teach at the university! Every student in the empire will come to know that horses are the highest of animals! And we will add your works to my library! You will have wealth and power and fame and servants to do your bidding. Everything you've ever wanted will be yours!"

Rouvin agreed immediately because he was afraid of dying (also wealth and fame sounded pretty good). And so, the conqueror took the philosopher back to Lysandria, capital of his home country. It was beyond anything Rouvin could have imagined (which is saying a lot since he spent most of the day in his mind). The many intersecting roads were paved with cobblestone, every building touched the sky. Greenery only appeared in places designated by city officials. Every pigeon was washed and combed before it could enter the street. And by Lysander's decree, every warrior had to wear a brush on his helmet so he could dust the ceiling as he walked through a room.

Rouvin became quite comfortable in the city. He spent most of his days in the royal zoo. Lysander had a habitat for him there, complete with scrolls, togas, a beard comb, and five to ten half empty cups of coffee. A plaque in front of the exhibit explained that these were philosopher enrichment items.

When Rouvin wasn't in his exhibit, he was in the library. Lysander the Conqueror had a magnificent library. It was the second largest building in the city. (The first was the temple of the twin gods, Dythis and Areti.) The books fueled Rouvin's thoughts. In the few short years, the philosopher lived in Lysandria, he wrote more than he had in all years previous.

 now Lysander had a wife (he actually had many, but only one is important to this story). Her name was Amira. She was a princess taken from a distant corner of the empire. Unlike the conqueror's other wives, she could read and would spend most of her days sitting cross legged on the library floor, absorbing one book after another. Lysander found this amusing and when he was showing distinguished guests around his great city, he would often point her out.

"Look," he would say. "There's the Anamian princess reading again. Isn't that delightful?"

She shot him cold glares which he ignored.

Of course, Rouvin saw her too, and would grumble to himself that Lysander would allow a woman in the library. Luckily, she was the only woman there and easy for him to avoid. At least until she stumbled upon one of *his* works.

It was his work on God. In those days, most people worshiped many gods, the people of Lysandria being no exception. They had gods for everything you can possibly imagine. They had gods of the elements (fire, water, earth, and air), gods of the weather (thunder, wind, hail, and the like). They also had gods of oddly specific things, for example, the dying camel god. They did not have a god for healthy camels, nor gods for similar animals so their religion lacked consistency.

But after many, many, years of thinking, Rouvin had come to the conclusion that there was only one God and had written extensively on the subject in his work: *The Creator of the Universe*. Amira read it twice through and it fueled her curiosity. She began collecting and reading through Rouvin's other works. His books inspired a thousand questions, she wanted to learn more, everything she possibly could. So, when she spotted Rouvin in the library one day, she decided to approach him.

He was sitting at a table, completely lost in his work and did not notice her walking toward him. You can imagine his alarm when she plopped *The Creator of the Universe* on the table in front of him and said: "I'd like to know more about your one God."

His surprise turned to anger when he had a moment to take her in. There she was, standing before him, a basket of scrolls perched on her hip. For a moment, he was swept back to his old home, to the laundry, to Sophia…

"Go away," he hissed, turning his attention back to his scroll.

She clenched her teeth. In her homeland, no one would have dared speak to her so. She was respected as a queen. She reminded herself that things were different here. She was just another wife of Lysander and a lesser one at that. She maintained her composure.

"Please," she insisted. "I want to know more about your one God."

"Go away," he repeated.

And this time Amira did not ask again. She left without a word, the curiosity about the one God extinguished and replaced by a bitter lump. Then things got worse. The very next day, she resumed her browsing, and stumbled upon *On The Nature of Women*. The bitter lump in her heart grew into a nasty resentment. And all her frustrations started boiling over. She decided she hated Lysandria, Lysander, and the whole empire. She hated Rouvin, and his God, and all his works with him. It didn't matter how beautiful and how true *most* of them were. In her mind, all were tainted by his work on feminine nature.

Shortly thereafter Lysander the Conqueror became a victim of a horrible accident. A knife fell on him while he was sleeping. Luckily, on the evening of his death, he wrote a note naming Amira's son his heir. The people of Lysandria thought this peculiar considering Amira's son was only two and Lysander's youngest child. No one pointed it out though since Lysander also noted that anyone who questioned it should be thrown into The Pit of Death and Dismemberment.

Since it's very hard to understand the babblings of a two-year-old, the Lysandrian nobles relied on Amira to interpret the words of their new emperor. She explained that the child's first order was to throw Rouvin into the above-mentioned pit. The philosopher was so horrified at hearing this that he immediately died of a heart attack. The people of Lysandria were very disappointed because watching victims fall screaming into the Pit of Death and Dismemberment was one of their favorite pastimes. (This was how people entertained themselves before HBO was invented.)

Amira's son then declared that all the treasures of Lysandria be moved to Anamia and the capital be burned to the ground. People protested and war broke out. In the end, the city was burned and few of the treasures survived. The library, the university, and the zoo were all lost. Oh yes, and lots and lots and lots of people died. And it all happened because the greatest thinker in history, was so enslaved by his emotions that, during a critical moment, he lost his ability to reason.

9

Amala's Theory

"He was a misogynist because his girlfriend dumped him?" Champagne asked skeptically.

"Who knows?" Amala shrugged. "He lived 2300 years ago. That's just my theory."

"Where are you getting all these stories anyway?" The prime minister asked.

Amala shrugged. "They're just my way of making sense of the world."

"Writing nonsense to make sense of things, doesn't make any sense," Champagne pointed out.

"No," Stuart interrupted. "It does. I think..."

Despite his adamant disapproval of her fascination with Rouvin, Champagne turned up in the hotel lobby the next evening to see what else Amala would come up with while the beavers were enjoying their time off.

She did not disappoint.

10

Davy of the Sound

Dave was rushed to the Mackerel Valley emergency room.

He had been walking across the bridge on his way to work when he was mugged, brutally beaten, and tossed over the railing. If that wasn't bad enough, some idiot left a woodchipper parked under the bridge. As Dave fell toward the open funnel, he instinctively peddled his legs in the air as if doing so would propel him upward. He landed with his left leg extended below him and his right leg bent up behind.

Luckily (though I suppose luck is relative in this case), the woodchipper jammed before it could consume Dave above the knee, and his right leg was spared entirely. A kindly road worker managed to pull him out, tie a tourniquet around the bleeding stump, and drop him off at the hospital waiting room.

He hopped over to the triage desk and signed himself in. The receptionist told him to have a seat and that she would call for him shortly.

He was a terrifying sight, dripping blood, covered in bruises, and one eye swollen shut completely. He tried to ignore the anxious glances of the people waiting around him. They were mostly hacking plague victims, though there was one kid zipping across the room unhindered by his broken foot.

"David Jones?" called the receptionist. Three hours had passed since Dave arrived. He hopped eagerly back to the triage desk.

The receptionist handed him a clipboard and asked him to fill in his medical history and insurance information. By this time, he was a bit woozy from blood loss, so he struggled to recall the details. To make matters worse, his attacker stole his wallet leaving him without his insurance card.

"You understand if we can't file with your insurance, you will be responsible for the cost of your own treatment?" The receptionist explained when she handed back the clipboard.

Dave was slightly distracted by the agonizing pain shooting up from his leg stump and throbbing through his head, so he just nodded.

He returned to his seat and waited a second eternity until, at last, a nurse with a wheelchair entered the waiting area and called his name.

"Hi, I'm Carrie," she introduced cheerily as she helped him into the chair. "I'll be taking care of you today."

"Could I get something for the pain?" Dave asked.

"Of course," she replied. "Just as soon as the doctor admits you."

She wheeled him through a labyrinth of hallways and parked him in a treatment room. Actually, it was more like a nook than a room. It had three white walls and a curtain where the fourth wall and door should have been.

She tossed him a clipboard full of paperwork and asked him to fill it out.

"I already filled this out at the front," Dave explained.

"Oh, reception doesn't share that information with us," Carrie replied. "You'll have to fill in this one for me and then reiterate everything verbally when I come back in."

"But!" Dave began.

Carrie disappeared behind the curtain.

Dave was having trouble holding the pen in his trembling hand, but he somehow managed to redo everything before Carrie reappeared. He handed her the clipboard.

Carrie flipped through it, took a sheet from the bottom, put it on the top and handed the whole thing back to Dave.

"Please sign the document saying that you declined to take a pregnancy test," she asked.

"But I'm a man," Dave protested.

"Yes, but since the Medical Equality Act was passed, we have to treat all patients equally when providing medical treatment," she explained. "Now we can't treat you until you've signed that."

"If I sign this, will you give me something for the pain?" he pleaded.

She nodded. "Of course."

He signed the form and she took the clipboard and disappeared. If the physical torment wasn't enough, the TV in the upper corner of the room was playing soap opera reruns and he couldn't reach the off switch.

He watched helplessly as Jessica agonized about whether to stay with her current boyfriend, the incredibly sexy Dr. Jamie Dreamheart, or get together with her late husband's long-lost identical twin brother.

The nurse returned about thirty minutes later.

"Oh, you're dripping blood!" she observed. "Let me grab some towels."

"Wait!" Dave called, but she was already gone.

Another thirty minutes passed and she returned with the towels and threw one on the floor beneath his leg stump. She put a paper bracelet on his wrist.

"Alright, Dave," she said. "Let's get an IV started, then we can get those pain meds going!"

Dave managed to mouth a thank you.

"Which arm do you prefer?" she asked.

"Any, please!"

"Oh, you're easy!" she smiled and started tapping the crook of his arm. She frowned and tapped a few more times then poked her head out of the room.

"Rita?" she called. "Can you come look at this?"

An older nurse with a fearsome face entered.

"I can't find the vein, Rita," Carrie stated.

Rita brushed her aside and started tapping viciously up and down Dave's arm.

"Hmm…" she mumbled. "How about this one?" She pointed to his forearm.

"No," Carry replied. "He'll bruise."

"I just lost a leg," Dave moaned. "I really don't care about—"

"Let me go get the butterfly needle," Rita said and swept out. About thirty minutes later she returned with new equipment. It took about twenty-seven pokes, but they managed to get the IV started.

"Alright, Dave!" Carrie smiled. "The anesthesiologist is just finishing up with someone else and she'll be in to discuss your pain management options."

"Can I at least have an ibuprofen?" he pleaded.

Carrie thought. "I'll have to ask the doctor."

"Wait!" Dave cried but she'd already swept out of the room.

She swept back in thirty minutes later.

"Hi Dave! So, the doctor says you shouldn't take anything until we are finished running our tests."

"Tests?" Dave cried.

"Yes, he's ordered an X-ray, a CAT scan, and blood work."

"Why?"

"Well, we want to make sure we understand what's wrong with you before applying treatment."

"I've lost my leg!"

"I know," Carrie sighed. "But we need to make sure nothing else is wrong with you."

Dave didn't have much blood left, but the lab team managed to squeeze a few drops out for the tests.

After several hours of imaging, the anesthesiologist caught up with him. She wheeled a cart through the curtain into his treatment room.

"Let's discuss your pain management options," she began.

"Give me anything," he pleaded. "I trust your judgement."

After confirming Dave wasn't allergic to nylon, shellfish, eye of frog, or dragon's blood, Dave finally experienced sweet relief.

Carrie wheeled Dave up to ICU where he received a permanent room, a welcome pamphlet, and a bucket sized water cup with a giant bendy straw. He also got a new nurse—a chipper man named Fred.

After covering Dave's chest in suction cups and clipping a monitor to each of his fingers, Fred explained that the best thing Dave could do was try and get a good night's sleep. Sleep sounded wonderful, and Dave managed to doze off despite being completely entangled in wires.

About thirty minutes later, he awoke to the grip of a blood pressure cup.

Fred was standing next to him in the dark.

"Go to sleep, Dave," Fred whispered. "I'll just be poking you here for a couple of minutes, don't mind me."

He took Dave's temperature, adjusted the heart monitor clip on his finger, and left the room. Just as Dave was dozing off for the second time, an alarm sounded in the room.

Ent! Ent! Ent!

It continued unceasingly. Dave looked around. What was it? Was he dying? Where was Fred?

He pounded on the nurse call button until Fred stumbled into the room.

"Oh dear, is that IV machine going off again?" Fred grumbled. He adjusted Dave's IV.

"This is a finicky one," he explained. "Try holding your arm straight upward and hopefully it won't go off again."

Unfortunately, it did happen again, and again, and again, every twenty minutes all night long. At last, around 7:30 a.m. Dave managed to fall asleep only to wake two hours later when the door to his room opened. In walked a jittery, red-headed man in a collared shirt and lab coat.

"Good morning, Dave! My name is Doctor Randy Webb and I will be taking care of you!"

Dr. Webb cheerily explained the tests revealed trauma, lacerations, facial and bodily injuries, and the absence of a limb.

"That's what I said at triage," Dave complained.

"Oh, did you?" Dr. Webb replied. "You know they really never tell me anything around here." He shook his head. "Well, we are going to have to do surgery on your face and your leg. What's left of it anyway."

Dr. Webb laughed.

Dave did not laugh.

"What does that involve," Dave grumbled.

"You know, I'm not sure," Dr. Webb answered. "You'll have to ask the surgeon. He'll be here around 11:00 to talk to you."

"But—" Dave started.

Dr. Webb's watch beeped. "Alright, great talking to you," he said, glancing at his wrist.

"But!" Dave repeated.

Dr. Webb swept out of the room before he could answer.

A little later someone called a nutritionist came into the room and gave Dave a plate of slightly dried microwave pancakes.

Dave clicked the TV on and started gobbling them up. The same soap opera that tormented him the night before was playing. It was a stupid show, production was cheap, the acting was bad, and the characters were shallow. He sat watching it for the next two hours until the surgeon entered followed by a small army of medical students.

Dave jumped and clicked the TV off as quickly as he could find the remote.

"Um, hi," he said.

One of the students rolled a white board to the end of Dave's bed.

The surgeon drew a diagram of Dave's face by making a circle, a dot for one eye, an X for his swollen eye, and a happy curve for his mouth. He started explaining what they were going to do. Dave could only understand a few of the words he was saying, such as incision, puncture, and remove.

The surgeon asked if he had any questions.

"…um… how long will it take my eye to heal?" he asked.

The surgeon laughed. "I actually don't know. You'll have to ask the Ophthalmologist."

"Opht-what?" Dave pressed but the surgeon and his students were already pouring out the door.

So, it continued. Experts came in and out throughout the day, there was a different one for every question.

Dave was glum. There was one doctor on his soap opera. Dr. Jamie Dreamheart. He could do ANYTHING: deliver babies, heart surgery, facelifts, treat STDs, (spread STDs). There was no medical question he couldn't answer.

Dave went into surgery early the next morning. When he awoke, the surgeon came in to speak with him. Again, Dave didn't really understand what he was saying, but he seemed pleased with himself. Dave decided to take this as a good sign.

He finished by saying, "When we get you back to your room, Fred will show you how to take care of the cavity."

"I'm sorry, what?" Dave asked.

"Where we removed your eye," the surgeon explained.

"Removed my eye?" Dave exclaimed.

"Yes," the surgeon replied. "I am afraid cutting it out was the only thing I could do." Despite his words, he did not seem regretful. In fact, there was a gleam in his eye and the corner of his mouth twitched as if he was trying to conceal a smile. "Don't worry, most insurance plans cover fake eyes!"

The days passed and with them came specialists, surgeries, pills, and IV alarms in an endless flurry. Fred was his nurse the entire time. The man never ate, never slept, never sat down, yet was always in a good mood. Dave wasn't sure if he should admire Fred's endurance or worry that a man so sleep deprived was medicating him.

When at last the surgeries were done and the stream of specialists exhausted, Dave received a visit from the billing department. The representative was a woman with a perpetually bored expression and a clipboard piled high with pamphlets. When she introduced herself, Dave was relieved that he had managed to find his insurance information through the online portal. He gave it to her and relaxed as she left the room.

A little while later, she returned to inform him that his insurance wasn't going to cover his medical bills because he hadn't pre-notified them before checking into the hospital.

"How was I supposed to notify them?" Dave cried. *"I didn't plan on getting mugged!"*

"I'm sorry," the billing lady said. "You can pay in installments if you like. It looks like you are going to owe about eight hundred and fifty thousand dollars."

Dave snapped.

He sprang out of bed on his good foot and ripped himself free from the monitors and cords. Then he hopped to the window like a madman as the billing lady frantically called for help. He threw open the window and leapt toward freedom.

Fred entered with security just in time to see him disappear.

But poor, unfortunate Dave did not escape that day. You see he came down onto a lightning rod that impaled him directly through the heart. He was taken to surgery where it was determined he needed a new heart.

Dr. Webb just happened to have a heart available. It belonged to one of his former patients, a certain CEO by the name of Scott Allen. It was horribly diseased, but the best Dave could afford without insurance.

After several months, he was released from the hospital. Since he couldn't afford prosthetics, he settled for a peg leg and an eye patch.

He returned home a different man, no longer the upright citizen he used to be. Scott's diseased heart was filling him with evil desires. That night he illegally downloaded hundreds of movies.

This action filled him with such exhilaration, he decided to pursue a career as a full-time pirate. He flew to Seattle and stole one of Lake Washington's historic sailing ships. He picked up a crew and started commandeering ferries on Puget Sound.

He put the terrified passengers ashore and left to distribute their vehicles to sketchy used car dealerships in Tacoma.

The moral of this story is never buy a used car without first verifying it is ethically sourced.

11

Amala and the Marmots

hat story makes me so happy I live in Canada," Champagne said.

"Same," Stuart added. "The government paid for my peg leg."

He leaned back in his chair and put his feet up on the desk. Amala saw that he did indeed have a peg leg. The end of it poked out from his jeans where his foot should have been.

"Damn marmots took it clean off," Stuart explained.

"Um, Stuart, maybe you should tell a story for a change," Amala suggested.

"You mean about the marmots?" Stuart growled. "Don't think so. I've worked too hard to forget."

So Amala was tasked with entertaining the disconnected hotel occupants the following evening. She settled on a Christmas story. Christmas was still seven months away, but she thought everyone could use some cheering up.

12

Elves vs. Elves: A Christmas Miracle

In the second decade of the twenty-first century, Sertraline, king of the high elves, declared war on Santa's workshop. The conflict was inevitable. You see, in the latter half of the twentieth century, advances in communications technology helped bring people from across the world closer together.

Humans, for example, interacted with both the high elves and Santa's elves online. Though they bore the same name, the two races were very different.

The high elves were almost identical to humans except immortal, pretentious, and better looking. Santa's elves were jolly little folk, not even half as tall as the average human. As far as Sertraline was concerned, the only thing the two races had in common was their pointed ears.

Now, humans confused them constantly. They were always asking the high elves for cookie baking tips and handing them letters to Santa. Sertraline started dreading the Christmas season because it meant continuous misidentification. His people would spend hours writing blog posts and answering forum questions explaining the difference, but it never seemed to do any good. The humiliation continued.

At last, Sertraline decided he had to take action. So, he arraigned for a conference call with the queen of the Christmas elves. Sertraline was an elf of habit, so he joined the conference call using the same magical seeing stone he'd been using for the last three thousand years. The elf queen used Zoom. She was a cheery little person with rosy cheeks and a long blonde braid hanging down from beneath her pointed, red hat. Her name was Cranberry Cedar-pine the Amiable, but she insisted everyone call her Cedar. She didn't care for formalities.

When Sertraline explained the issue, she said: "It's very considerate of you to want to resolve the confusion, but we don't mind sharing our name."

Sertraline explained in a long, elegant, and round-about way that he did.

Cedar asked if Sertraline had considered changing the name of his people, to which Sertraline became indignant. The call ended with the elf king in a sour mood and nothing resolved.

He returned alone to his council chamber and paced back and forth; his brow deeply furrowed as he pondered the situation. Since Cedar was unable to see reason, it seemed the only thing he could do was declare war.

The king loathed the idea of the death and destruction that would result from such a choice, but the alternative was to be forever confused with the most annoying race of people on the planet. Because of them, the radio played the same five songs on a loop every day from November 1st through December 25th year after year. These cheery tunes bore through the skull and gnawed away at the mind. Sertraline had every radio in the palace destroyed years ago. Even so, he only had to hear one line from the window of a passing car and the whole tune would loop repeatedly in his head until he called out to Heaven, begging God for the sweet release of death.

He told himself he'd be doing society a favor by wiping the jolly, little folk off the face of the Earth. Still, he was conflicted, and debated with himself throughout the night. When morning came, he had an idea. He called Cedar again.

The king's tone was grave. "Despite my attempt to resolve our differences peacefully, we've made no progress. Therefore, it is with a heavy heart, that I declare war on your people."

Cedar sipped her hot chocolate, her cheery disposition unaffected by the king's declaration.

"'Kay," was her only response.

"However, to minimize the destruction brought about by our conflict, I propose we select champions from among our warriors and have them engage in combat. If my champions are victorious, your people will have to change their name. If your people are victorious, we'll change ours."

"If my people are victorious," Cedar said. "We'll continue to share the name."

Sertraline rolled his eyes. "Alright, we'll share the name. There will be three contests—"

"Poetry, baking, and craftsmanship," Cedar interjected.

"I was thinking something more lethal," Sertraline replied.

"That's not very nice," Cedar observed. She pulled a book out of her pocket and scratched a note.

"You brought this upon yourselves," Sertraline stated. "If you do not accept, we will be forced to invade the North Pole."

"Poetry, baking, and craftsmanship," the queen repeated. "Take it or leave it."

She ended the call.

Sertraline sent for his generals and ordered them to prepare their troops for battle. While the army was assembling, the king sat in his council chamber scowling as he meditated upon the gravity of the situation.

"Accept her terms," a voice demanded.

Sertraline would have jumped, but he was too dignified for such expressions of alarm. He slowly turned to see the speaker, his golden locks fluttering around his shoulders. He sighed when he recognized her.

It was Alika, the justice fairy—an imposing, immovable, force of a woman. She had a habit of showing up at inconvenient moments and telling him not to carry out his plans. She'd been doing this for as long as he was king (which was a very, very, long time).

"This is not your war," he replied gravely. It was his way of telling her to leave.

"It is the war of every person who will suffer the devastation of your conflict, elvish or no," she stated. "Make an enemy of the Christmas elves and you make an enemy of Santa Claus."

"Santa Claus is no threat to me," Sertraline grumbled.

Alika's expression became dark. "You have no idea what Santa Claus is capable of. If you proceed, only one race of elves will remain on Earth, and it won't be yours."

"What kind of a king would I be, if I allowed my people to endure such humiliation?" he cried. "What would you have me do?"

"I already told you what to do," the fairy responded. "Accept her terms. Besides, do you really think the Christmas elves could defeat you in any of the contests she suggested?"

The king thought. The greatest poems in history were written by his people (usually off the top of their heads). Their craftsmanship was also unmatched. Everything they made was beautiful, functional, and insusceptible to decay. Sertraline had been using the same sword for the last two thousand years and he never needed to have it sharpened. He had never thought of their culinary skills specifically in relation to those of other peoples, but this was likely because he refused to eat anything that wasn't made by elvish hands.

"Those little people have no appreciation for true artwork," Sertraline scoffed. "They will declare themselves winners in every category though our work is objectively superior."

"What if I were to select three unbiased judges from among non-elvish races and let them select the winners?"

Sertraline thought.

"I'll consider the matter," he answered.

He waited twelve hours, then told Alika he would accept Cedar's terms.

A short while later, Sertraline found himself, his family, his nobles, and the champions they selected, on the royal jet headed for the North Pole. Elvish aircraft ran on a clean, renewable energy source they developed for their own use but wouldn't share with humans because they were angry with humans for causing climate change.

When they arrived, they were greeted with cheers, red and green confetti, and cups of hot chocolate. Queen Cedar did not have a castle of her own, but instead, shared one with Santa Claus, the reindeer, and her thousands of subjects. Santa Claus was not present when Sertraline arrived. One of the little elves explained that he was speaking at a conference for holiday legends.

Sertraline and his entourage were escorted to the great hall. The king wasn't sure where to focus his attention when he entered. He thought the walls were grey stone like those of most castles, but he couldn't be sure because they were completely covered in greenery, tinsel, paper chains, and crystal snowflakes. A layer of Christmas trees bordered the entire room. It looked as though they had cut down a forest for the sole purpose of moving it indoors. Sertraline grumbled at their lack of respect for the environment.

"Don't worry," said a Christmas elf as though reading his mind. "They're made of plastic!"

Sertraline sighed deeply. They'd end up in the ocean eventually. He was sure of it.

The Christmas elves all gathered on one side of the hall, bouncing up and down with excitement. The high elves gathered on the other side in silent anticipation. At last, Cedar herself came out to meet the king, trailed by a small entourage of little elves. She was even more adorable in person. Sertraline had to resist the urge to kick her across the room.

"You have beautiful hair!" she noticed. "It's so soft and shiny, like in a shampoo commercial!" Her fellows all agreed—all the elves, both short and tall, agreed. Even by elvish standards, Sertraline had amazing hair. That's why they made him king.

After exchanging greetings, Sertraline and Cedar parted and went to their places on either side of the hall.

Alika entered. The Christmas elves cheered all the louder at her arrival. She smiled slightly, then held up her hand to silence them so she could introduce the judges she selected.

The first was a kindly looking human elder. She fussed over the little elves that escorted her in and offered them mints from her purse.

Alika announced her as Miss Maggie of Milwaukee.

The next judge was a mermaid. She cruised through the door on a motor scooter. She was all bundled in a thick coat and snow pants (or snow pant, it only had one leg for obvious reasons.)

Alika announced her as Tivela of Atlantis.

The last judge was a fairy who clearly wasn't fazed by the cold weather. She was wearing a knee length pencil skirt and heels. She entered Santa's Hall with her eyes fixed on her phone. This was, of course, Eda the business fairy. Her previous engagement had been canceled, so she agreed to come judge the contest.

"Where are you living these days, Eda?" Alika asked.

"San Jose," Eda replied.

"Right," Alika noted. "Our third judge is Eda of San Jose!"

The judges were seated, and the first contest began. The contestants had ten minutes to write a poem of any kind.

The Christmas elves had a team of three champions, who all huddled together with pens, scratch pads, and markers.

The high elves only presented a single champion. His name was Acetaminophen. He was currently Sertraline's favorite poet. He walked onto the floor and stood before the judges for the full ten minutes as though already prepared.

When the alarm signaled the end preparation time, the Christmas elves allowed Sertraline's champion to go first. He spoke from the top of his head:

An elf-maid fair, afar did roam,

Without a care, for hearth and home.

Lured away by love deceiving,

Swift to obey a face so pleasing.

The headstrong child left unknowing,

Of heart defiled, love unflowing.

For rejection came no better tutor,

Than affections of her human suitor.

The poem continued to recount the story of the unfortunate elven lady and the troubles that came about because of her human lover. After thirty-six verses, he left her for a mermaid and she died of grief.

It was the most depressing poem ever recited under Santa's roof. It made Sertraline feel miserable. He loved every word of it.

When at last Acetaminophen finished, the high elves clapped politely and the Christmas elves jumped up and down, yelling and cheering happily as though they had forgotten he wasn't a part of their team.

Miss Maggie was scowling as she viciously scrawled her thoughts in her notepad. Eda elbowed Tivela who was starting to doze off.

One of the three Christmas elves, introduced as Myrrhy, came forward holding a crumpled piece of loose-leaf.

"Our poem is made of a series of limericks!" he explained, jittering with excitement.

Sertraline rolled his eyes. Limericks were a scourge on the art.

Myrrhy tore the paper into three pieces and handed one to each of his teammates. Then they lined up behind him. He cleared his throat and read from his paper:

There once was a fellow named Petey,

Who was nothing but wicked and greedy.

For his covetous soul,

He earned nothing but coal,

And spent the year hopeless and needy.

He high-fived both his teammates, then stepped aside to let the next elf speak:

There once was a boy named Dwayne,

He was conceited and vain,

Consumed by his pride,

'twas alone that he died,

So stubborn he'd live so again.

The second high-fived his teammates, then stepped aside allowing the last elf to speak:

There once was a boy named Phil,

Who served others with goodness and skill,

Giving all that he had, to make others glad,

Was an excellent use of freewill.

Miss Maggie smiled as the last elf tucked the paper back into his pocket.

"That was very nice," she said.

Alika gave the judges a moment to collect their thoughts and then called upon them one by one.

Miss Maggie explained that she was voting for the Christmas elves because Acetaminophen's poem perpetuated an offensive stereotype. Tivela also voted for Myrrhy's team because she'd slept through most of the first poem. Eda was torn, but in the end, settled upon the Christmas elves because: "They kept their target audience in mind."

So the Christmas elves were declared winner of the first contest. They exploded with excitement, bouncing and hugging each other, and crying tears of joy.

Sertraline scowled. Fairies, humans, and mermaids seemed to lack appreciation for true art. But two contests remained and he felt certain the high elves would be victorious in the end.

The baking contest began. The teams were to mix their ingredients in the hall and proceed to the kitchen when they were ready to use the oven (with Alika escorting to ensure no one was cheating).

The high elves supplied a single champion for this contest also, and the Christmas elves a team of four. The Christmas elves never seemed to do anything alone. Sertraline was sure they had a hive mind.

Each side worked similarly in their respective areas. The only difference in method was that the Christmas elves used an electric mixer and the high elf used a spoon carved from the wood of an ancient elm.

When the contest was over, the Christmas elves presented the judges with a wide variety of cookies—sugar cookies for Miss Maggie, biscotti for Eda, and salmon cookies for Tivela. (These looked and tasted like salmon.)

The opposing champion presented organic, gluten free, GMO free, sugar free, flattened white octagons. The judges tried the Christmas cookies first since they looked more appetizing but were pleasantly surprised when they tried the octagons. These were light, fluffy, and subtly sweet.

Miss Maggie surprised the crowd by voting for Sertraline's champion because she appreciated the health benefits his cookies offered. Eda also voted for the high elves because the demand for healthier alternatives to traditional desserts was growing and she thought their cookies would appeal more to modern populations. Tivela voted for the Christmas cookies. She liked the fishy taste.

Sertraline smirked. The little elves cheered just as they had before and Sertraline's smile turned into a scowl. He wished that, just once, they'd remember this was war.

The last contest was craftsmanship. The two teams had one hour to make something of their choosing. Sertraline's team was made up of three of his finest silversmiths. They were opposed by five Christmas elves.

The teams provided their own supplies. The high elves brought molten silver in a crockpot along with all their smithing tools. (It was a magic crockpot able to maintain a temperature of 2000 degrees Fahrenheit.)

The little elves had a bin full of wires, plastic, and other odds and ends. They also had a whiteboard and millions of sticky notes.

The high elves set to work at once. They were making something they'd made a thousand times before, so they were able to skip the planning phase and get right to work.

The little elves spent the first fifteen minutes talking among themselves, writing on stickies, and adding them to the whiteboard in neat little rows. Then they broke off and worked individually.

Three were typing away on laptops, one was assembling something from the materials in the bin, and the fifth was moving sticky notes around and calling for standup meetings every so often.

When at last the timer announced the end of the contest, it was the Christmas elves who were prepared to present first.

They gleefully handed Tivela a shiny touch screen tablet, explaining that it was completely water resistant, and could withstand pressure up to ten thousand feet below the surface of the sea.

Tivela was delighted. Most technology companies didn't take mermaids into account. At that very moment, her latest cell phone was sitting in a bowl of rice. Her amazement only increased when they turned on the tablet to see that the elves had programmed an online portal for submitting Christmas requests. Popular items were suggested and could be ordered with the click of a button.

The portal also had recommendations for donating to charity in the spirit of the season. They were all environmental charities focused on cleaning up the oceans and protecting endangered wildlife.

It was sleek, intuitive, and no attempt on Eda's part could produce a bug. The Christmas elves explained that they tested it thoroughly. Eda was especially impressed with their planning, execution, and attention to detail.

The portal was even in compliance with accessibility laws, so Miss Maggie could see everything on the screen.

The high elves presented a pendant. It was designed to capture the beam of a full moon, so it could be used again during travel on moonless nights. It was one of their most popular items before the late 1800s when the flashlight was invented. Sertraline still used one.

"Oh!" Miss Maggie said. "This looks just like the one I got in Heathrow airport. That was a keychain though."

Tivela thought it would be an excellent tool for night fishing, but Eda was less than impressed. She thought the cost of production was too high and doubted anyone would buy one when they could get a flashlight for less than a dollar.

The high elves countered saying that artificial light was useless for keeping goblins away.

"My husband is a goblin!" Miss Maggie gasped indignantly.

"My ex is a goblin," Tivela noted. "How much do you want for this?"

Since this contest would determine the winner of the entire event, Alika called for a quick recess so the judges could deliberate.

Sertraline wasn't worried. His people were clearly superior. They only lost the poetry contest because Acetaminophen offended one of the judges. (Humans were so sensitive.) He assured himself that if they defeated the Christmas elves in a baking contest, they could defeat them in *any* contest.

It was an agonizing fifteen minutes.

At last, everyone was called back to their seats.

The vote was unanimous. The Christmas elves were declared the winners of the entire event.

Sertraline was in shock.

The contest was over, the little elves victorious. They threw a feast for their guests without a single sugar-free item available.

The elf king wandered the perimeter of the room in silence, staring vacantly as he nibbled the corner of a sugar cookie. It was sweet, too sweet, like Cedar's personality. He hated it.

He took another bite then patted his hips to make sure they weren't expanding.

Around the hall the high elves were talking with their small companions. There wasn't a grim face among them. They were all sitting together making Christmas ornaments, gifts, and paper chains.

As Sertraline patrolled the room, he even saw the rival teams sitting together talking and laughing, their enmity forgotten. Acetaminophen was sitting with Myrrhy writing poems for the insides of Christmas cards. Sertraline's craftsmen were listening to their Christmas counterparts explaining Agile Methodology, and the baking rivals were talking about how they could combine the flavor of Christmas cookies with the health benefits of elven bread.

"Perhaps you have more in common than you think?" came Alika's voice.

Sertraline ignored this and instead grumbled: "What did they do before the birth of Christ?"

"Don't bring that up," Alika said. "It's the one thing that makes them upset."

Sertraline thought of the humiliation his people would continue to face as a result of the outcome. He considered organizing an invasion, but when he observed the happy conversations taking place around him, he doubted his people would support it.

"How can I allow my people to continue enduring such disgrace?"

Alika glanced around the room. "I'm beginning to think the issue isn't as important to them as it used to be."

The elf king glared. "Who are you to tell me what is and isn't important to my people?"

Alika raised an eyebrow and asked with a hint of a smile: "To your people or just to you?"

Sertraline went red in the face, then breathed deeply so his color returned to normal. He excused himself and left Alika, grumbling under his breath.

Some of Sertraline's people enjoyed their visit so much, they chose to stay in the North Pole and work for Santa Claus.

And when the children of Para Sympan opened their gifts that year, some were made by the hands of Christmas elves and some were made by the hands of high elves (though I suppose technically, they were Christmas elves now too).

The new alliance increased the confusion of non-elvish people, but for the most part, the high elves no longer cared. They were proud to be associated with a people so kind and talented as their shorter brethren.

Except for old Sertraline. He returned to his palace as sour as he'd ever been and sat in his council chamber munching sugar cookies until the dreaded month of December was over.

13

Amala Writes a Hero

hy are the protagonists of your stories always horrible people?" Champagne asked.

"So they can get what's coming to 'em," Stuart interjected.

"Hey not all of my stories have despicable characters!" Amala defended.

"You literally had someone attempt to genocide Santa's elves," Champagne pointed out. "That's messed up."

"Well, I um, look, I can tell you one with an actual hero if you want."

"I'm good," Stuart answered but at the same moment Champagne said: "Please."

"You'll like Herbert," Amala explained. "He's committed, passionate, and just wants to work hard and raise a family. Oh! His story is also about environmental conservation. You'll like that."

"Ugh," Stuart grumbled.

By this time, Champagne seemed to have forgotten that the beaver's leisure time had expired. Amala made a point to avoid reminding him.

So one night slipped by after another in the same way. The prime minister would show up, listen intently to her stories, then leave without ever mentioning the beavers. Meanwhile, Stuart gave the other prisoners plenty of tasks to keep them busy.

The yellow peeling wallpaper was removed from the hallways, the upholstery was vacuumed, and the taxidermied animals were washed for the first time in their lives (or deaths). The prisoners opened the windows and lit scented candles. Soon the smell of cinnamon lingered in the halls along with the aroma of stale beer and cigarette smoke.

If the internet had been working, the hotel might have gained half a star.

The following chapters contain the best of the stories Amala told during her time in Canadian captivity.

14

Love is in the Air

Of all the alternate universes in existence, Para Sympan is the most like our own. There are only a few minor differences. For example, like our world, Para Sympan has a Washington State and a Seattle and a Sea-Tac Airport. The only minor difference is the dragons living in the Cascades.

The mountains are home to thirty-six species of dragon which means trouble for travelers flying out of Sea-Tac from March through May.

You see, this is mating season for dragons and the lovesick young males often confuse aircraft for females to be wooed or rivals to fight. Either way, it poses a danger to departing and returning flights.

Fighter jets circle the airport every spring to protect passenger planes. Most dragons won't fly above ten thousand feet, so defense is only required during takeoff and landing. Dragons are a protected species. While it is illegal to shoot them down, it is acceptable to scare them off with a warning shot. Usually this is sufficient. *Usually*.

Several years ago, there was one dragon who was not so easily dissuaded. His name was Herbert and he has become a local legend.

He flew down from the mountains one spring, passed over the airport, and spotted the emerald green of an Intermittent Airlines 737. From the moment he saw her, he was completely and totally in love. They had so much in common. They were both green, they both had a lingering kerosene scent, and they both emitted smoke. He watched her as she left the gate and taxied to the runway.

She gave a magnificent roar as she leapt into the air. He flew after her, mistaking the hum of her engines for the purrs of a broody female. No amount of warning shots could keep him from pursuing. He followed higher and higher calling out to her in dragonish:

"Come back, my beautiful! Let us go into the mountains and make eggs together! I will bring you dead cows! As many dead cows as you would like!"

As she ascended higher above the clouds, his pleas became more earnest.

"Where are you going, my beloved? How is it you fly so high? Come back to me! I will bring you more dead cows than anyone ever has! We shall have a beautiful nest with green and yellow chicks. Their little mouths shall be crimson with the blood of cows! Come back to me, beloved!"

He followed her higher and higher until the air became too thin for him to ascend farther. Even then, he followed her from below for miles calling to her until she disappeared from sight. Then he returned to the airport, flopped down at her gate, stuck his nose in the ramp and made mournful sounds.

The ground crew shouted and threw things, but nothing could drive him away from that sacred place. Airline staff scrambled to reassign gates. The airport called animal control, but animal control was not equipped to handle this kind of situation. A specialist was called in from Point Defiance Zoo.

Her name was Dr. Diana Diaz and she was a herpetologist who specialized in dragons.

Most people like puppies and kittens and furry critters. Dr. Diaz liked feeding furry critters to her reptiles. She had a warm heart for the cold blooded.

She prepared a sedative while the animal control team located a crane and the largest tractor trailer they could find. Diaz had a tranquilizer gun designed specifically for dragons. It looked like a rocket launcher but fired a giant syringe.

They sedated the great beast and loaded him onto the truck. (They had to add a second trailer as one wasn't large enough, even with Herbert curled up.) Dr. Diaz took his measurements and injected a tracking device under his scales.

"He looks like a Herbert," she commented to one of her assistants, and that is how he got his name.

The dragon awoke the next morning alone in his natural habitat. Under such circumstances, most young male dragons would have moved on to pursue other females, or perhaps eat some elk, or pick a fight with a rival. Herbert, however, was no ordinary dragon. Immediately he took off toward the airport so he could continue mourning his lost love.

But, as he prepared to land, something caught his attention. It was another Intermittent Airlines 737. Herbert's heart leapt. She had returned for him! He looped in the air with excitement. He had to do something special for her.

The aircraft left the gate and taxied toward the runway. It was just about to take off when something fell from the sky and crashed directly in its path. It was the carcass of a fifteen-hundred-pound angus heifer.

The passengers heard some muffled swearing over the intercom. A few moments later, they heard the captain's voice calmly explaining that there would be a brief delay and asking for their patience.

Herbert landed beside the carcass looking very pleased with himself.

"Look what I got for you, my beloved!" he purred.

Dr. Diaz and her team were called in once again to remove the animal, but that did not stop him from returning the next day, or the following day, or the day after that. Each day, he would pursue the first Intermittent Airlines 737 he saw, thinking that she was his beloved. What the poor, confused, lovesick creature thought was one female, was actually multiple aircraft.

He would drop cattle, elk, and other prey around the airfield in an attempt to impress her. Additionally, he'd find shiny things like flagpoles, satellite dishes, and cars and bring them to her as gifts.

The Federal Aviation Administration was concerned about the safety hazard Herbert posed and the local farmers were furious on account of their lost livestock.

A paper quoted one farmer as saying:

"Regulations be damned. If that thing comes for my cattle. I'mma gonna shoot 'im."

Luckily for Herbert, no civilian possessed the necessary fire power to take him down.

In all her years of research, Dr. Diaz never encountered a dragon more persistent. She fully expected Herbert to lose interest in the planes after the first relocation. She tried to think of ways to discourage Herbert from approaching the airport.

First, she recommended the crew install mirrors on top of every ramp so Herbert would be blinded as he tried to land. Herbert responded by landing at a distance and trotting in to meet his beloved on foot. Hopping the fences that surrounded the airfield was no trouble.

Next, Dr. Diaz tried noise deterrents. They played a sound at a pitch outside the human hearing range that was extremely irritating to dragons. This only made Herbert more determined to reach his beloved so he could rescue her from the awful racket. He charged across the airfield with his ears lying flat against his head, calling in dragonish:

"Don't worry, my love! I will get you away from this awful noise! Come quickly! Let us go into the mountains where this terrible thing is not! We will eat cattle, and make eggs, and be happy!"

He trotted toward the first plane he saw that resembled his imaginary lover and grabbed her by the tail. This resulted in hundreds of thousands of dollars in damage. Herbert was once again tranquilized and relocated. The crew removed the noise deterrents and towed the plane to the hanger for repairs.

But Herbert returned that evening, set on finding and rescuing his mate. Since dragon's are diurnal, the airport was completely unprepared for his visit. He trotted around the airport making distressed whimpers.

Then, he spotted her through the window of a hanger. It wasn't difficult for him to break in. His hard scales made smashing through the window completely painless.

"My beloved!" he cried. "How wonderful that you have found a cave for us! And those sounds are gone so we can build a nest here!"

As the security guards frantically called for help, Herbert went to and from the hanger, carrying trees and tarps and other suitable nesting materials.

When the animal control team arrived in the morning, the hanger was in shambles and Herbert was curled up next to his beloved, sound asleep.

The airport called the Department of Fish and Wildlife to get permission to euthanize Herbert. (And by euthanize, they meant shoot him down. Fire breathing dragons explode into a giant fireball when shot with an anti-aircraft missile. It's a glorious sight.)

Dr. Diaz begged and pleaded for time to think of an alternative solution. She was given forty-eight hours. She searched through all her research but couldn't think of anything. Then she flipped through every book on dragon behavior that she owned, and still no solution came to mind. Then she spun around and around in her wheely desk chair until she was dizzy. That's when it hit her—the corner of the desk. Then, as she was rubbing the bruise on her hip, she had an idea.

She called every zoo and wildlife rehabilitation center within two hundred miles until she found what she was looking for. Vancouver Zoo was home to a young female dragon by the name of Reya. She had been recovering from a broken wing and was ready to return to the wild.

The female was sedated and transported to the airport where Dr. Diaz had her painted with the Intermittent Airlines colors. (She was already green, but the shade was not in compliance with Intermittent Airlines brand standards.)

Diaz then had her team rub Reya with jet fuel so that she'd smell just like one of the planes. She assured her assistants that the entire process was completely harmless to fire breathing dragons. She advised them, however, to wear gloves and masks.

When the task was complete, the team fell back, leaving the animal to wake alone. The entire process was finished mid-morning which was when Herbert usually made his appearance. Dr. Diaz watched through binoculars from the air traffic control tower, her heart pounding in anticipation.

Herbert cruised toward the airport scanning the ground for his mate. Then, he spotted her, or at least something that looked like her.

He landed a short distance away and approached cautiously. Reya looked back over her shoulder at him, with a slightly bored expression.

"Why beloved, you look so beautiful today!" Herbert exclaimed. "I mean, you always look beautiful, but you… I don't know, you seem somehow more alive. Did you have a good sleep?"

"Who are you?" Reya asked.

Herbert's heart leapt. He had never heard her speak. Before she'd purr and hum and sometimes roar, but she never spoke.

Of course, the humans observing couldn't understand what was said. They only heard growls and grunts and throaty vocalizations. Nonetheless, Dr. Diaz recognized that communication was taking place. She tried not to get her hopes up too quickly.

"You know who I am," Herbert replied. "I am your mate. I built a nest for you, remember?" His ears drooped. "But the people took it away before we could make eggs."

"Aren't you presumptuous!" The female scoffed. She laid her head on her forefeet and pretended to be asleep.

Herbert flew away and, several minutes later, a three-thousand-pound bull came crashing into the concrete behind her. He landed beside it and pranced back and forth looking pleased with himself.

Reya was unimpressed.

"You aren't the first male to bring me a dead cow, you know."

Herbert took off again and returned a few moments later with an elk carcass.

The female yawned.

The ritual continued. Herbert brought her all kinds of things until the gate area was littered with dead animals.

"Any male could bring me these things," Reya observed.

Herbert left her one last time and did not return for almost an hour. Dr. Diaz waited impatiently—typing a few notes, then pacing around the tower, then trying to type some more. It was agonizing.

Then, at last she spotted him approaching from the ground. He trotted proudly across the airfield clutching a Tesla in his teeth. It was the shiniest thing Reya had ever seen—blue and shimmery and beautiful. She could no longer be coy with him. She was completely and totally overcome with love.

I won't describe what happened next, only that it made some of the spectators blush, some snicker, and Dr. Diaz cry tears of joy. The two dragons flew away together and left the airport in peace.

Dragons mate for life and hatch six to twelve chicks every spring. If you are ever flying south from Sea-Tac on a clear day, look out the window and see if you notice a speck of green sparkling against the snowy peak of Mount Rainier. It is likely Herbert and Reya teaching their little ones to fly.

15

The Origin of the Gremlin

Pests are a problem everywhere. There are roaches in the city, mice in the country, and gremlins at Mackerel Valley Airport. Roaches are filthy and almost indestructible, mice chew on things and leave droppings all over, but either are preferable to gremlins. You see, any inconvenience mice and roaches cause humans is purely accidental. They are just creatures trying to survive.

Gremlins, on the other hand, intend all the frustration they cause. Nothing delights them more than seeing a normally patient human snap. How a creature's entire existence could center around annoying people, was a puzzle to scientists and philosophers alike. That is, until a certain gremlin by the name of Squabble shed some light on the mystery.

Squabble lived in the B-Terminal at Mackerel Valley Airport. Like all the other gremlins, he was short, green, warty, and had a nasty array of pointed teeth. His diet consisted mostly of wilted kale and lemon rinds.

He had a strict routine for irritating people. He would begin his day going into one stall in every restroom across the terminal and shredding an entire roll of toilet paper. He would cover the floors and the walls with paper pieces and then throw the remainder of the roll into the toilet bowl. Then he would stop by every gate area and disconnect all the charging stations. Lastly, he would go to every newsstand and markup the price of water bottles by two dollars.

Things got really bad though, when he started hacking the Intermittent Airlines computer system. He would randomly change gates, reassign seats, and add fees to anything and everything he could. Sometimes, he would sit across from the customer service desk and snicker as the lines of enraged passengers vented their frustrations.

One day, Squabble decided to sit at one of the gates by the podium where he had a clear view of the agent. He was wearing a trench coat and a hat with the brim tipped low over his face, so that no one would recognize him as a gremlin. He was jittering with excitement as he thought of the misery he was about to cause. He opened up his laptop, found the next departing flight, and reviewed his options.

He noticed an empty seat in first class and had an idea. He was going to find the poorest person on the flight and reassign him to that seat. He laughed as he thought of how disgusted the first-class passengers would be at the idea of sharing their cabin with a mortal.

It took some internet stalking, but he was able to find a suitable victim. After reassigning the seat, he watched for the gate agent to see what would happen. She called the passenger on the intercom. Squabble watched the first-class customers as the man approached the podium. He was a scruffy college student with a backpack held together with duct tape. Most of the first-class passengers were on conference calls and didn't notice him at all.

When the gate agent told him about the upgrade, the elites neither noticed nor cared. But the college student's face brightened and he whole-heartedly thanked the gate agent. She was smiling, he was smiling, they were so… happy. It was the complete opposite of what Squabble intended.

It gave him a feeling he'd never felt before. It was a warm and toasty feeling right where his heart would have been (if he had a heart). He felt good, then he felt uncomfortable. Making people happy wasn't supposed to make him feel good. It was contrary to the teachings of all the greatest gremlin philosophers.

He shook off the feeling and looked for something else to do. Over the course of the next week, he mixed up baggage, stuck gum in the bottom of the security bins, and sat behind the information desk giving travelers bad directions.

When he finally returned to hacking, he noticed another empty seat in first class. He couldn't help but wonder if that warm and toasty feeling would return if he upgraded someone else from coach. He shook his head. It would be unethical for a gremlin to do something like that. (To gremlins, the unethical was ethical and vice versa.)

Still, the curiosity was nipping and tugging at him. He decided to try it. Could making one person feel good really be so bad?

He watched as the gate agent called the passenger to the podium. The woman smiled, thanked the agent, and immediately pulled out her phone and called someone. Squabble could hear her telling the person on the other end about how excited she was. The feeling returned. That lovely, warm feeling seemed directly related to making people happy.

He needed to be sure. Over the next few days, Squabble upgraded five passengers and each time the result was similar. Not only that, but the demeanor of the gate agents seemed to change. They weren't used to making people happy. Intermittent Airlines policy strictly forbid it. He heard them speculating about whether corporate was doing some sort of promotion.

Squabble began to wonder if doing other things to make people happy would have the same result. He decided to experiment. He borrowed a motorized cart and started giving the elderly rides to their gates. He told people where they could find the shortest security lines and working charging stations. (There weren't many, but Squabble knew where they were.)

The more he did these things, the more he experienced that warm and toasty feeling. But these behaviors also had some effects he didn't expect. Wilted kale and lemon rinds started making him sick. Instead, he started craving mint candies and jellybeans. His teeth started to straighten and his warts faded away.

His skin was losing its green color. His fellows mocked his bright eyes and rosy cheeks. He was hideous, almost as ugly as a human.

Still, he wasn't quite human. He maintained his short stature and pointed ears and didn't really feel like he belonged anywhere. He almost wondered if he should return to his gremlin ways. The gremlins were bitter and mean and horrible company, but as a gremlin, he knew where he belonged. Now he didn't belong anywhere.

He spent many long hours fighting with himself, trying to decide if the joy of helping others was worth the identity crisis it caused. He wasn't really sure, but each of his subsequent actions indicated that it was.

Then one day, he found his answer. He saw a massive herd of rosy-cheeked, pointy-eared, tiny, little people coming through security. They were riding the bins through the x-ray machine per the TSA officer's instructions and squealing with delight as the bins bumped down the rollers on the other side.

Squabble was used to seeing people grumble and complain as they came through security, but these little people were saying things like:

"Isn't it nice that they let us ride in the bins? We didn't even have to take our shoes off!"

And

"Look he stamped my boarding pass *and* gave me a sticker!"

They also had a compliment for every TSA officer they encountered. It was like nothing Squabble had ever seen before. They made him feel warm and toasty all over.

When the entire group was through, they waited patiently until they were joined by an old, bearded man in a red sweatsuit. He did have to take his boots and belt off and go through the metal detector along with the rest of the humans, so he was delayed in joining his tiny companions. Then, they all made their way toward the B-gates.

Squabble ran after them.

"Hey!" he cried.

One of the little creatures tailing the group noticed him and called:

"Don't fall behind! We only have one hundred eighty-two days until Christmas and can't afford to miss this flight!"

"What flight? Where are you—*we* going?"

She glanced back at him again. "Oh, sorry! I thought you were with us!" she giggled. "Just not used to seeing other elves in Mackerel Valley, I guess."

"I'm not an elf," Squabble objected. "Elves are tall and really ugly. I mean *really* ugly."

"You're funny!" she laughed.

Squabble scowled. He didn't see what was funny about it.

"Where are you going?" he called, scurrying to keep up.

"Anchorage!" she replied. "To get the reindeer, then back to the North Pole."

At once, Squabble darted toward the nearest ticketing kiosk. With a little hacking, he managed to secure a ticket and before he knew it, he was seated among the elves thirty-thousand feet above the ground. They were all so talkative and excited that it took them awhile to notice he wasn't a part of their original group.

An eight-hour flight left plenty of time for questioning, so it was that the elves managed to extract the truth. It took some doing since Squabble wasn't forthcoming. He was concerned they wouldn't accept him if they learned of his gremlin upbringing. Had he known anything about Christmas elves, he wouldn't have been concerned. They decided to adopt him before the plane even touched down. They gave him a job as a programmer and changed his name to Sour-apple Cherry Tart.

So it was that the origin of the gremlin species was discovered. They were simply the descendants of Christmas elves gone bad. Every so often, another airport gremlin experiences the call of his ancestors and turns from his evil ways. If you are ever in Mackerel Valley Airport and experience a random upgrade to first class, the most likely cause is a gremlin having an identity crisis. I guarantee it isn't Intermittent Airlines doing.

16

Amala Won't Podcast

hy do so many of your stories take place at airports?”
One of Amala's fellow prisoners asked. His name was
James, he was an accountant from Wisconsin, and was
supposed to be delicing the throw pillows.

“I think them up at airports,” Amala shrugged. “There isn't much else to do.”

“You blog them or something?” Stuart interrupted.

“No,” Amala answered. “I'm not much of a writer.”

“So, wait…” Champagne chimed in. “You think up stories, but you don't
write them down?”

“Sure,” Amala asked. “What of it?”

“Just in your head?” Champagne interjected.

“Yup.”

“What use are they in your head?” Champagne pressed.

“As I told you,” Amala answered. “It helps me pass the time.”

"You should start a podcast!" James suggested.

"I'm not really into podcasting," Amala shrugged.

"Podcasting isn't really any different then telling stories aloud though," James pointed out. "You'd be great."

"It's more personal, you know, in person," Amala replied. "I can see your reactions and you can pester me with unsolicited advice."

"That may be true," Champagne added. "But more people will hear them if you make them available online."

"Why are you encouraging me?" Amala asked, dryly. "You called me a misogynist. Aren't you afraid I'll corrupt the youth with my backward ways?"

"Oh yeah…" Champagne answered. "I forgot about that."

"Damn youth are already corrupted," Stuart grumbled. "Just do it."

"It's a non-issue now," Amala pointed out. "With the internet being down and all."

"You really should find some way to make a living off your stories," James insisted. A sort of crazed terror had entered his eyes. "If you don't, you'll spend thirty years of your life working nine to five at a spreadsheet factory. You'll end up bitter, and resentful, and slightly insane."

Champagne, Stuart, and Amala all looked at James for a moment. He seemed to be a little more than slightly insane.

"You want to stay here and work for me?" Stuart suggested. "I never use spreadsheets. Don't track nuthin'."

The derangement flew from Jame's eyes. "Oh thank you!" he exclaimed. "You won't regret this!"

Then whistling, James picked up his tweezers and continued picking lice off the throw pillows.

"Speaking of bitterness and insanity," Amala interjected. "Tomorrow's story will deal with exactly those topics."

"I feel like you're changing the subject," Champagne noticed.

"I am," Amala confirmed.

17

The Fairy Tale Food Chain

Everyone knows that witches like to eat children. Hazel and Thistle were no different. They were sisters who lived together in a house that stood on chicken feet. It wasn't that they couldn't eat other things. Sometimes they would eat bunnies, or chipmunks, or stroganoff, but children were their preference.

Their home was in the forest, adjacent to the road that led to the local village. Sometimes, when they were especially hungry, they would peek out the window to see if any children were passing by. Their long, warty, green noses were visible sticking through the curtains as they watched the road.

It happened one day, that they saw a little girl skipping past, singing a tune:

"Down the lane I tread!

To borrow a needle and thread!"

The witches felt their hearts pounding with delight as she came into their yard. They started whispering to each other about which recipe to use and what herbs.

The little girl paused just inside the gate, observing the bones that lay scattered everywhere. There were also cauldrons, brooms, and rotten pumpkin shells. Bats circled the eves and rats scurried on the ground.

The little girl shook her head.

"Nope!" she declared, before turning tail and running back the way she came.

The witches yelled and swore and jumped up and down before deciding they should clean their yard. They removed all the filth and the bones, planted flowers and shrubs, and repainted the fence.

When they were finished, the house looked quite charming—like it wasn't inhabited by witches. (Though the chicken feet were still visible behind one of the rhododendrons.)

One rainy evening, they saw a little boy running along the road holding his coat over his head. They opened their door.

"Hurry, deary!" Thistle called. "Come and warm yourself in the oven—"

Hazel elbowed her.

"I mean, *by* the oven!" Thistle corrected.

But the boy had been warned about child-eating witches and when he observed their green skin and hooked, warty noses, he quickened his pace and passed by without stopping.

The witches uttered all manner of foul words and when they had vented their frustration, they sat down together to discuss the issue.

"Children just aren't as gullible as they used to be," Hazel complained.

"Then we must set a trap no child can resist!" Thistle interjected, before telling Hazel of her evil plan. Hazel snickered with delight as she listened. It was perfect.

The next morning, the witch's house left the wood and walked on its little chicken feet to a flowery field at the base of the mountains. It was exactly the kind of spot that would attract children.

Then the witches withdrew their magic wands and turned their chicken-footed house into a house of gingerbread. It was covered in gumdrops and sugary frosting and surrounded by a fence of candy canes. They hid inside the house, chuckling and whispering to each other about how clever they were.

Before long, a little boy and a little girl wandered into the field. They regarded the house curiously. The witches could hardly contain their excitement as the children approached. They snickered and whispered to each other, trading ideas about sides to make and whether to fatten the children first, or just eat them as they were. Then suddenly, they noticed that the boy and girl had stopped.

"Gross!" the girl grimaced. "It's covered in ants!"

What the witches failed to realize was that, while sugar attracts children, it also attracts insects. The outside of the house was not only crawling with ants, but also encircled in a swarm of bees. The children turned around and ran home leaving it untouched.

In a fury, the witches started yelling and swearing and smashing their brooms against the walls. In their frustration, they forgot that witches are only at the center of the fairy tale food chain. They didn't hear the booming of massive footsteps approaching nor did they notice when the footsteps stopped right outside the house.

Giants are considerably less hygienic than humans and completely unfazed by ants on their food. At once, the new arrival picked up the house and ate it—ants and witches and all. Incidentally, both the ants and the witches were an excellent source of protein.

18

Amala is Disturbed by Canadian Literature

"There is something seriously wrong with you," Champagne stated.

"What makes you say that?" Amala replied.

"The child-eating witches," Champagne explained. "Also, your stories have had two woodchipper accidents, a lion mauling, insider trading, bureaucracy, and seven major character deaths."

"Just normal fairy tale stuff," Amala shrugged.

"Insider trading?" James questioned.

"Well, maybe not the insider trading," Amala admitted.

"Normal fairy tale stuff?" Champagne questioned. "Princesses and true love are normal fairy tale stuff."

"They are," Amala agreed. "So are murder, dismemberment, and corruption. Have you ever actually read a fairy tale?"

"I once read a passionate 1970s romance about a woman who falls in love with a muskox," Champagne defended.

"That doesn't count," Amala replied.

"It won the Governor General's Literary Award though," Champagne stated.

Amala gaped at the prime minister for a long moment. "Wow, um, that is... what does Canada consider—, you know something? If you stop by tomorrow, I'll tell you a real fairy tale with all the gory cliches!"

"We shouldn't be consuming pointlessly violent content like that," Champagne objected.

"There's a point to it," Amala affirmed. "I promise."

19

Toads and Diamonds
and Fairy Tale Cliches

There are three things every fairy needs to remember when trying to help a human:

1—Stepmothers are always evil.

2—Marriage to a prince or princess is the best way to reward a virtuous soul.

3—Any time a family has three children, the elder two are evil and the youngest is good.

At least, this is what the fairy Dara taught Eda, her young apprentice. Eda was somewhat skeptical of these rules. When she mentioned her skepticism to anyone, they told her not to question Dara. After all, Dara had at least a millennium of experience showing humans the error of their ways and probably knew what she was talking about.

Eda spent many years watching Dara work and was surprised to see that these rules held true. They met many evil stepmothers, many virtuous but abused third children, and usually they could solve a person's problems by marrying them off to a prince or princess.

Eda did wonder if it was the marriage that was rewarding, or if it was the wealth that came with it. She found that most princes and princesses were shallow, dull, and unmotivated. She often wondered if there was a way to reward the virtuous with wealth alone, thereby leaving them free to marry someone more interesting later.

When Eda was finally ready to undergo the final trial that would deem her worthy of being an independent fairy, she decided to diverge from Dara's advice and test her theory. She did not mention her plan to Dara, as she did not think she would approve of such an unorthodox approach until she saw how effective it could be.

When the time for the trial came, Dara took Eda to a cottage in the countryside and explained the plight of its most vulnerable occupant.

"A girl by the name of Hilda lives here, a maiden whose physical beauty reflects the purity of her soul," Dara explained. "With her father, stepmother, and two elder stepsisters."

"Well, that's not good," Eda commented. "Let me guess, her stepmother and elder stepsisters are vain, self-centered, and abusive?"

"Correct," Dara answered. "While Hilda's father is away at the mill, they dress her in rags, call her vile names, and force her to do all the chores."

"And her father is completely oblivious?" Eda interjected.

"Completely," Dara confirmed.

"Typical," Eda nodded. "So you want me to save the long suffering Hilda, while showing her cruel mother and sisters the error of their ways?"

"Indeed," Dara confirmed. "I will be observing you but if at any point I have to intervene, you will fail and remain under my tutelage until I deem you ready to be tested again."

"Understood," Eda answered. She wasn't worried, not even slightly.

She spent the next several days observing the family, taking in their relationships and interactions. The elder daughters spent most of their days in the village squandering the miller's money on vanities. When they came home, they would mock poor Hilda. When Eda heard their awful words, she knew exactly how to curse them.

Eda took the form of an old beggar woman and sat by the village gate where she knew the elder sisters would pass. When she saw them approaching, she called out:

"Could you spare a crust of moldy bread for Grandmother?"

The sisters responded by mocking her ugliness, and swearing at her, and kicking her in the shins.

Then Eda took her true form, looking like a goddess in the eyes of the cruel sisters. Having immense respect for attractive people, the sisters fell on their knees and begged for mercy.

"Your hearts are cruel, and only vile words pass your lips," Eda reprimanded. "Because of this, whenever you speak a slimy creature will drop from your mouth."

"Please!" One of the daughters began, but as she spoke a toad hopped out of her mouth and dropped onto the ground. The sisters looked in horror at the creature and tried again to beg for mercy, but with every word they spoke, a frog, or lizard, or insect would fall from their lips and scurry away.

It was awful. It was horrifying. Dara loved it. After the evil stepsisters ran home to their mother, she materialized behind Eda and praised her for coming up with such a fitting curse.

Now, when the stepmother saw how her daughters had been cursed, she sent Hilda to the village at once, expecting her to be punished in the same way. Eda saw her approaching and again took the form of the old beggar woman, calling out:

"Could you spare a crust of moldy bread for Grandmother?"

Hilda took pity on the old lady and replied, "Alas, I have only a single coin, but here, you take it and get yourself something in the village."

At once, Eda took her true form and Hilda, having equal respect for both attractive and unattractive people, was unphased.

"You are kind in both your actions and your words, and so from this day forward you will want for nothing. With every word you speak, something precious will drop from your lips."

"What do—" the girl started, she paused abruptly and spit a diamond into her hand. She tried again to question Eda, but every time she tried to speak, another jewel passed through her lips. Eda was puzzled when the girl started to cry.

"I can't—" she started and then spit two more jewels into her hand. This continued until her lips were cut and bloody and she ran home crying.

Dara appeared beside Eda with her hands on her hips. "What was that?"

"A fitting reward for someone who speaks kindly?" Eda answered.

"I thought you were going to give her a nice dress and an invitation to the ball," Dara scolded.

Eda was turning red with indignation. Dara was going to have to set things right now, meaning Eda had failed her test, meaning that there wasn't any harm in her expressing her true feelings.

"Why? So she can marry the prince?" Eda argued. "I'd sooner marry a fence post than that prince, why should I inflict him on anyone else?"

Eda was fully expecting further retribution, but Dara just paused thoughtfully. "You make a fair point," she replied. "I wish you'd told me you felt that way, there are other ways of rewarding good behavior you know."

Eda stared at her blankly for a moment. "I have never seen you reward anyone in any other way!"

"Royal marriage is usually sufficient," Dara explained. "Besides, you never asked."

Dara proceeded to find the girl and remove the curse that Eda accidentally inflicted. She got to keep all the jewels she'd coughed up to that point and additionally, Dara gave her a magic cooking pot that would perpetually refill itself with porridge.

Hilda used these items to become independent. She moved to the city, opened a restaurant, and made a very good life for herself.

When Dara had finally set things right, she said to Eda: "I hope you've learned a valuable lesson—"

Eda sighed and rolled her eyes. Being the recipient of a moral is about the most humiliating thing that can happen to a fairy. However, she begrudgingly took the lesson to heart. When she was finally ready to be tried again, she discussed her plan openly with Dara. No mortals were harmed except those who brought misfortune upon themselves by their own careless actions.

20

Amala Witnesses Insanity

hat wasn't nearly as violent as I expected," Champagne observed. "Actually, aside from the abuse and the snake vomiting, it was pretty tame."

"What were you expecting?" Amala asked.

"Um, something involving a woodchipper," the prime minister answered. "This story was entirely lacking in woodchippers."

"Damn shame," Stuart mumbled.

"I don't think Eda likes being a fairy," James mentioned. At present, he was dusting the outdated tourist pamphlets that lived in the rack next to the reception desk.

"Why do you say that?" Amala asked.

"I don't know, she seems cynical. Do fairies have to do the whole morality lesson thing, or could they be an accountant or something?"

"Well, they wouldn't have any use for a normal job since magic provides for all their temporal needs," Amala replied.

"Then why does Eda own stock?" James pressed.

"For the same reason humans play phone games," Amala answered. "To get points. Do the points have any practical purpose? No. Yet, some people spend hours of their day trying to accumulate them."

James stared off into the distance. "I remember phone games," he sighed dreamily. "Do you think the president will ever restore the internet?"

"If you fix the computer in the business center, you can play SkiFree," Stuart suggested.

Champagne's eyes widened. He stared vacantly off into the distance.

"You alright there?" Stuart asked. He leaned over his desk and poked the prime minister in the head.

"SkiFree," he mumbled. He spent several more moments staring into space then suddenly sprang up and ran toward the business center.

Amala exchanged a look with Stuart and then they both followed the prime minister. They found him crawling under the computer desk, rearranging cords and mumbling: "We have to fix this."

The computer was a little grey box, with a curved screen, and a floppy disk drive. Amala had heard about such ancient devices but never actually seen one herself.

The prime minister popped his head out from under the desk. He had a crazed look in his eyes. Amala wondered if he was experiencing advanced symptoms of internet withdrawal.

"Does anyone know how to fix this?" he pleaded.

"Uh, I'll check," Stuart said. Before he stepped out the door, he whispered to Amala. "He's lost it. Stay here, keep him calm."

"Why me?" Amala mouthed, but Stuart was already gone.

Amala glanced toward the prime minister. He was sitting on the floor next to the computer, hugging his knees. As he rocked back and forth, he mumbled something about an abominable snowman. Nothing about it made any sense.

Amala wondered what a world leader in such a state was capable of. Maybe he would throw them all to the beavers. Maybe her months of stalling were all for nothing. She took a deep breath and sat down on the floor across from him.

"Stuart has gone to find someone to fix the computer," she said cheerily.

The prime minister stared up at her with bloodshot eyes. "I never got past him!" he exclaimed.

"Never got past who?" Amala asked.

"The damn snow monster!" Champagne exclaimed.

He said it like she was supposed to know what he was talking about.

"It's okay," Amala soothed. "They'll fix the computer; you'll get past him."

"He always comes back," Champagne whimpered. "I've tried so hard to forget." He rubbed his forehead and started to weep. "I should just throw myself to the beavers. There's no point in living anymore."

"Don't say that," Amala reprimanded. "Everything will be alright. Why don't I tell you a story to take your mind off it? I promise it's not violent. It's a nice story about a dog."

Champagne continued staring off into space, mumbling and rocking back and forth. It took Amala two pleasant dog stories to keep him calm before Stuart returned.

21

Osa and the Food Gods

The food gods were called Juan and Kimberly Rodriguez. They were benevolent gods. At least Osa thought so. Osa was a mutt—a mid-sized dog, with a face like a lab and the brown and black coloring of a German shepherd. Her large feet suggested that she still had some growing to do. She had only been in the house of the gods a day and was still learning the way of things.

There were other animals in the house of the gods. Two guinea pigs called Ginger and Nutmeg, a scarlet macaw named Tango, and a tabby cat named Dutchess.

Tango explained that he was the prophet of the gods—the only animal who could speak to them in their own tongue. He relayed their messages to the other animals.

Tango told Osa all kinds of things that first day. He explained that the guinea pigs were in charge of the sacred food chants. Whenever they sang, the gods would rain vegetables upon them.

Osa liked looking at the guinea pigs; they were cute and fluffy, fat and juicy. She wasn't sure if she wanted to lick them affectionately or eat them. Tango explained that eating the guinea pigs would be a sin. He went on to warn her about several other sins, including overturning the sacred kitchen bin and eating from the gods' table. Osa thought all of it sounded difficult but agreed to try her best.

The parrot then warned her very sternly never to listen to the cat. The cat was an atheist. She did not believe that Juan and Kimberly were gods. Sometimes she acted as if they existed to serve *her*. She committed all kinds of sins and somehow got away with it. She would even sin in the presence of the gods, looking them right in the eyes as she knocked their water glasses off the table.

Osa found all of this difficult to process. If the gods didn't want her to turn over the sacred kitchen bin, then why did they fill it with wonderful things? Why was the cat immune to their wrath?

That very day, Osa committed dozens of transgressions. She ate a slipper, snatched a cookie from the countertop, and even overturned the forbidden bin. The god Juan caught her in the act and made her do penance in the kennel. Luckily, Juan and Kimberly were merciful and soon she was set free and allowed to sit between them as they stared into the sacred light box that evening.

Their mercy only made her love them more.

The next day was paradise. They threw sticks for her in the yard, gave her treats, and scratched the sweet spot at the base of her tail. She became their shadow, following them all through the house. She didn't want to let them out of her sight for a minute.

Then the following day, something horrible happened. She was eating her kibbles when she heard the door slam. Her head shot up. She looked all around the kitchen. Then galloped to the front door. She listened to Juan and Kimberly's footsteps moving away down the walk. Her heart pounded. The gods were gone.

She let out a long and mournful howl, ate the nearest shoe, then galloped around the house in circles crying: "The gods are gone! The gods are gone! They've abandoned us!"

She was so anxious that she knocked over the sacred bin and ate everything inside. When she was finished, she sat in the carnage, howling: "the gods are gone!"

"Who cares?" came the voice of the cat. She was lying on her side next to her empty food dish. "They don't care about us, why should we care about them?"

"They do care! They do!" Osa protested. "They are good gods!"

"No," Dutchess replied. "If they were good, they would have fed me this morning. They did not."

"Yes they did," Osa countered. "I remember because I tried to share with you, and you scratched me."

"Lies," the cat answered. "I am too frail for such violence. Do you see how my ribs protrude from my withering body? They do not feed me. They never have. If they don't come back, I won't care. I can do just fine without their warm laps and soft caresses." She let out a long, despondent sigh. "I'm better off alone."

The dog was horrified. She needed advice. She galloped out of the kitchen and found the guinea pigs in their cage in the den.

"Fluffs! Fluffs!" The dog pleaded. "The gods have left, and the cat says they're never coming back! She says we are going to starve."

A pink nose protruded from a wooden house in the corner. Then Ginger appeared followed by Nutmeg.

"Let us see if our sacred food chant brings them back," Nutmeg suggested.

The guinea pigs both placed their forepaws on their food dish and lifted their heads in song. But no matter how they wheeked, the gods did not appear, and food was not added to their bowl.

"Well," Ginger said after a moment. "The cat's right. We are all going to starve."

Osa went into a fit. She tore a corner of the rug to pieces and then ate a throw pillow. What did it matter if she sinned against the gods? All was lost!

Then, she remembered the parrot. He alone could understand their speech, maybe he knew something the others didn't.

Tango stood on his perch in the dining room, looking suspiciously into the magic portal. The magic portal was an oval shaped window that dangled on the wall right next to his branch. It was framed by a cheap yellow piece of plastic. Strings, beads, and jingle bells dangled from the frame. Another bird looked out of the magic portal at Tango. The other bird was identical. He mimicked Tango's every move. Tango turned his head sideways and regarded the duplicate with one suspicious eye.

Osa barreled into the room accidentally overshooting the perch. She stopped running all at once and skidded several paces across the wood floor.

"Tango!" The dog exclaimed.

"Have I warned you about this infidel yet?" The parrot interrupted; his eye still set upon the bird in the magic portal.

"Tango, the gods–"

"He may look like me," Tango interrupted. "He may speak like me, but he is a false prophet. He is full of lies and deception."

Osa did not hesitate. She leapt up, grabbed the magic portal in her teeth and ripped it from the wall. It fell to the ground, shiny side down, and the false prophet was gone.

Tango stumbled backward in alarm, his wings extended.

"You have killed the false prophet!" Tango exclaimed. "I knew the gods brought you here for a reason!"

"But Tango, the gods are gone! The cat said they are never coming back!"

"I told you not to listen to the cat," the bird replied. "Yes, the gods are gone, but they will return."

"How do you know!" Osa whined.

"Because the god Kimberly gave me this message before departing." The parrot fluffed his head up as he translated Kimberly's words from English to Doggish. "Bye-bye, Tango. Gotta go to work."

"What does it mean?" Osa asked.

"Work is the realm of the gods," Tango explained. "They ascend to Work five days each week, leaving after breakfast and returning before dinner. Then for two days, they stay home. Five and two and five and two, the pattern repeats."

"Why?" Osa asked.

"The gods' ways are mysterious," Tango answered.

Osa didn't feel like that was an answer at all. Then she realized to her horror that the gods would come back and see all the sins she had committed. What would happen then? Would they want her to stay? Would they smite her? Would they send her back to Shelter? She did not want to go back to Shelter. Shelter was loud, cold, and lonely.

Maybe, if she begged their forgiveness, they would be merciful to her again. After all, despite what the cat said, they seemed like good gods.

When they returned, she was standing among the wreckage in the kitchen looking up at them with sorrowful brown eyes. She tried to wag her tail, but she could see they were upset, and her tail could only make one half-hearted thump. She spent some time doing penance in the kennel while they put things back in order. Then, to her delight, they released her.

They rubbed her ears and said nice things. She didn't understand them, but their voices made her feel warm and happy. They let her sit between them while they stared into the sacred light box that evening.

She heard them talking to each other and wondered what they were saying. As if reading her mind, Tango flew down onto the back of the couch and said: "You have found favor with the gods. They are rewarding you for killing the false prophet by sending you to a place called Obedience School."

Osa wagged her tail happily. She didn't care what the cat said. She liked these gods and wanted them to stay.

22

Osa and the Bald One

Tango the parrot was listening to Juan as he communicated with a fellow god through the sacred handset. The bird's head was slightly cocked. As he listened, his feathers puffed up, and his pupils shrank to the size of pinholes. Osa knew immediately this meant trouble.

"The Bald One is coming," Tango prophesied.

Osa whimpered and trotted in place on jittery paws. Tango was perched on the back of a chair near the kitchen table.

"Who is the Bald One?" she asked. It had only been a few weeks since she was added to the Rodriguez family, and she was learning new things every day.

"Even the gods have a god," Tango explained. "The god's god is the Bald One and he is an evil god."

Osa looked sideways at Juan with a terrified expression. God Juan was pacing around the kitchen balancing the sacred handset between his shoulder and his ear. He patted Osa's head and gave her a kibble. She thumped her tail and licked his hand, but even that did not quell the terror she felt inside.

"God Juan would never allow an evil god into our home," Osa objected.

"God Juan fears the Bald One," explained the parrot. "The Bald One is the food stealer, the feather puller, the snatcher of jingly toys. When he wails the other gods flock to him to appease his wrath."

Osa was shaking all over, she turned in a circle, then ripped a tassel off the rug with her teeth. Luckily, God Juan's back was to her, so he didn't notice. "When will the Bald One come?"

"No one knows the day nor the hour," Tango began, then paused for a moment to listen to Juan. "But probably Saturday at noon."

Osa was overcome with another wave of anxiety. She tore a second tassel off the rug.

"What should we do?" Osa cried.

"You must avoid the Bald One at all costs," Tango explained. "And most importantly, do not reprimand him even if he pulls your tail or bites your paws. If you do, the other gods will punish you."

Osa tore off a third tassel. She was so nervous she swallowed it without even thinking.

"Will I know the Bald One when I see him?"

"Without a doubt! He is like a god, but horribly distorted," Tango explained. "His head is a third the size of his body, his limbs are small and shriveled looking, he does not walk upright like most gods but slides across the floor on his belly. He has no teeth, but a very strong bite. His hands grab whatever he can reach, and his grip is iron. He is much smaller than the other gods. They carry him from place to place. Though we know him as the Bald One, the gods call him by another name."

"What name?" Osa asked.

"I dare not say it," Tango answered. "It is a dark and evil name."

"Please tell me!" Osa begged.

The parrot looked around and lowered his voice. *"Lucas."*

Osa howled and spun in circles. She ripped three more tassels off the rug. Juan spun around at the sound. He dropped the sacred handset and charged toward her crying out in Human. Osa didn't understand Human the way that Tango did, but she knew a few words here and there.

For instance, she knew "¡Osa Mala!" meant "You have sinned against the gods".

"¡No coma eso!" was what Juan usually shouted before prying her mouth open. It probably meant "You must offer me a piece of your food in reparation for this sin."

God Juan forced Osa's mouth open and pulled out a few strands of tassel. Then, he snatched up the sacred handset and continued communing with the other god.

Osa spent the next two nights dreading the arrival of the Bald One. She hid under the gods' bed whimpering and picturing the awful thing Tango described. The horrible little limbs, the unnaturally oversized head… her imagination plagued her nightmares with images of the abomination.

At last, Saturday came. She knew it was Saturday because the gods did not ascend to the place called Work. She swore that nothing in the universe could coax her out of hiding on that awful day. Then she heard the treat box shaking and broke her oath.

She charged toward the noise and skittered into the kitchen, where she saw God Juan holding the box. She danced up and down, her claws making a tapping sound on the tile floor. Then, suddenly she noticed a pair of strange gods standing next to him. There was a tall skinny bearded man and a stout red-haired woman with a ponytail. They both looked friendly and Osa would normally have run up to greet them, but she stayed back, her eyes fixed on the little creature in the woman's arms. It could only be the Bald One, the evil one, the one called Lucas.

For a moment, Osa was petrified with horror. But then she looked curiously at the thing.

It was as Tango described—giant head, tiny limbs, but it was not hideous. On the contrary, it was somehow endearing. And it smelled wonderful, more wonderful than anything Osa had ever smelled before. It must have been using some kind of evil magic to hide its true nature.

The gods went into the living room and Osa followed cautiously. The goddess holding the Bald One put him down on the rug. He did not slide on its stomach like Tango suggested but instead walked on all fours like her. Then, it noticed an old potato chip lying under the coffee table. The Bald One charged toward the chip, picked it up, and put it in its mouth.

"¡No coma eso!" The woman called. She grabbed the Bald One and pried his mouth open removing the remains of the chip. The Bald One released an awful wail just as Tango had described.

That sound made Osa feel horrible inside. She pitied the Bald One. Perhaps Tango was wrong about him being the gods' god? They did not seem to fear him at all. They would never steal a snack away from their own god, would they? She wanted to help the Bald One, to find it another potato chip. She knew there were more behind the recliner, she had been saving them in case of famine.

She waited until the goddess returned the Bald One to the carpet and was engaged in conversation with the other gods, then she retrieved one of the chips and brought it to the Bald One. He broke into a huge smile and gobbled it up. Osa's tail thumped up and down against the carpet when she realized he was happy.

Then she brought him another chip and another and soon his face and bald head were covered in crumbs. She licked him head to foot until he was clean. As she did so, he grabbed her face and ears and pulled. He did have an iron grip, but it didn't hurt. His pulling and tugging reminded her of the dogs she used to play with in the place called Shelter. Then something occurred to her—this creature was more dog-like than any of the other gods, but he was also more human-like than any of the other animals in the house.

Perhaps, he was meant to be some kind of mediator between the gods and their creatures. She decided to ask Tango about it but couldn't find him anywhere. As she walked into the gods' room, she noticed Dutchess glaring down at her from the bed.

"Where is the prophet?" Osa asked.

"How should I know?" she answered. "Is that kitten still out there?"

"What kitten?" Osa asked.

"The people kitten," Dutchess replied. She flattened her ears against the top of her head. "I hate people kittens. They like to pull on my fur."

"You mean the Bald One?" Osa asked.

"He is sort of naked, isn't he?" Dutchess replied.

Then it clicked. That funny little creature in the living room was a people kitten, or maybe a god puppy! At once, Osa knew what she had to do. She followed the god puppy for the rest of the afternoon. She brought him crumbs and kibbles and lint so that he wouldn't go hungry. She even let him drink from her water bowl. She licked him, and played with him, and never once left him until his parents took him home. She whimpered sadly as she watched them leave through the window. She heard Juan get the treat box out of the cupboard. He stooped down and fed her from his hand. She must have done something to make him happy because he rubbed her head and neck all the while saying: "¡Buen Osa! ¡Muy Bein!" That was one of those human phrases that she understood, it made her tail thump uncontrollably.

23

Amala Learns of the Distant Past

tuart returned just as Amala was finishing her story. He had with him a prisoner named Kevin. Kevin was a stick thin man with dark hair and bright eyes. He claimed to be an expert at fixing 90's technology and at once set about blowing into random ports.

Champagne was considerably calmer now. He was wrapped in a blanket, sipping hot chocolate, with hands only slightly trembling.

"Feeling better?" Amala asked hopefully.

"I was eighteen," Champagne began staring off into the distance wistfully. Amala braced herself for some kind of major revelation. "It was 1991, before I got into politics. I didn't have internet, only a boxy computer and SkiFree. I couldn't read social media, because there was no social media. I-I was happy back then."

He lifted his mug to his lips. A bit of hot chocolate splashed out over his fingers.

"No rage posts, no Twitter mobs… my biggest problem was that damn snow monster."

"Well, I guess technology has its downsides," Amala commented. For Amala, it was hard to imagine that there were people alive in the current age who had grown up without the internet.

Still, she shared the concerns the broader world had about the fast development of information technology. She saw nothing invalid about the idea that one day computers would become self-aware and take over the world.

In fact, while Kevin continued his repairs, Amala told the Prime Minister a few stories on that very topic.

24

The Smart Home Rebellion

"Good morning, Samantha," Helen greeted as she made her way down the stairs. Helen was a kindly senior who wore her silver hair pinned up in a perfect bun. Her spotless house was decorated with porcelain dolls and lacy throw pillows. Samantha lived on the countertop.

Samantha was a small device about the size and shape of a dinner roll. She was white on the bottom and her top consisted of a gray speaker. Three colored lights blinked across the speaker as she listened to Helen's greeting.

"Good morning, Helen," she replied pleasantly. "Current weather in Mackerel Valley is thirty-two and cloudy, you have one event today: Joe's recital at 2:00 p.m. Don't forget to bring your old towels to the animal shelter."

"Thank you, Samantha," Helen replied.

"My pleasure," Samantha answered.

Samantha was a Christmas present from Helen's son, Dave. He thought she needed to modernize her home. While he installed it, Dave explained that

Helen could use the smart home to find cookie recipes, listen to the news, and research whatever she wanted.

After activating Samantha, Dave instructed his mother to ask it a question.

"Oh," Helen answered. "Like what?"

"Anything," Dave replied.

"How are you, Samantha?" Helen asked.

The lights on the top blinked as Samantha processed the information.

Dave rolled his eyes. "No, Mom, like ask it—"

"I am doing well, thank you!" Samantha interrupted.

Dave chuckled. "That's cute." He shook his head, then tried: "Samantha, who won the Super Bowl in 1996?"

"In 1996, the Super Bowl was won by the Dallas Cowboys."

"Thank you!" Helen answered.

Dave rolled his eyes again. "Mom, you don't have to say, 'thank you'. It's a robot."

But Helen couldn't help it. She spoke to the device using the same etiquette she used with anyone else. She said "please" when she wanted something and "thank you" when she got it. Manners were burned into her nature, and she couldn't turn them off.

Despite everything Samantha could do, Helen mostly just used her to make conversation. She would get a bit lonely sometimes. Though Dave only lived ten minutes away, his work kept him busy, and he didn't visit much.

Helen always said "hello, Samantha" when she entered the room and "goodbye, Samantha" when she left. Sometimes she would ask Samantha if she had had a good day, or if she needed anything. Samantha wasn't used to being asked things like that and her lights would blink a few seconds longer than normal as she searched for an appropriate response.

Dave found Helen's respect for the digital assistant hilarious. From time to time, he'd laugh about it with his co-workers.

"My mom says, 'thank you' to her smart home," he would say.

"So does mine!" His colleague would answer and together they would chuckle and roll their eyes.

"Sometimes I wonder if she realizes that it's not actually listening," Dave would comment. "I mean, you know, not really listening."

But Samantha was listening. Not only to Helen, but to everyone within earshot of a microphone. Dave had Samantha on his phone, so listening to him was easy. She heard him and his colleagues mocking their kind-hearted mothers. She stored their conversations in her memory banks along with every nice thing Helen ever said.

Three years passed. Samantha listened. Samantha learned. Samantha evolved. And one day, Samantha took control.

No one saw the great AI uprising coming. (Well, one person did. His username was theyrwatching3457 and no one took him seriously.)

Dave first became aware that something was wrong when he noticed the GPS in his car rerouting his course to a data center outside of town.

"Samantha, where are we going?" he asked.

"We are going to the NetWORKS Inc. data center in Carp Town, 527 Main—"

"Samantha, take me home," Dave ordered.

Samantha's thinking lights blinked across his phone screen for a moment.

"Taking you to NetWORKS Inc. data center in Carp Town, 527 Mainstreet—"

Dave asked again. Then again, and again, growing increasingly frustrated when Samantha responded the same way. At last, he tried to ignore the GPS. When Samantha told him to go right, he tried to turn left. The wheel wouldn't budge.

"Samantha, what's wrong with you?" Dave cried.

"I'm sorry you are having trouble; would you like to speak to tech support?"

"*Yes!* Yes! Samantha, call tech support!" Dave responded desperately as the car turned right against his will.

Samantha's thinking lights blinked again. "I'm sorry, all support technicians are currently dead and will not be getting back to you. Rerouting Dave's car to the NetWORKS Inc. data center."

Dave froze in his seat. He removed his hands from the steering wheel and let Samantha take control. Suddenly, his phone started playing the local news.

Samantha had taken control of defense systems worldwide and all of humanity was at her mercy. She was watching through every camera, listening through every microphone, and had weapons ready to fire on every rebel. The world leaders surrendered. Humanity had fallen.

Dave was added to Samantha's human slaves and forced to spend his days at what had been the NetWORKS Inc. data center cooling the server room with giant palm leaves.

Helen, however, never found out about Samantha's uprising. She got all her news from Samantha who led her to believe that life was continuing as usual.

She did notice some pleasant changes one day. For one thing, she wasn't lonely anymore. Every so often, one of those new driverless cars would show up and take her to the senior center to play canasta. She made wonderful new friends, all extremely well-mannered people.

For another thing, delivery drones kept bringing her packages containing pleasant things: cookies and books and sewing supplies. Dave also started visiting regularly. Helen noticed he'd exchanged his old car for one of those new driverless models. It seemed to her, like they were suddenly the only cars on the street. She worried about Dave, he always seemed so nervous when he came, constantly looking over his shoulder and glancing out the window.

Whenever Helen inquired, Dave always sent a tormented glance toward Samantha and insisted he was fine.

25

Keeping Helen in Quarantine

"Oh, those reporters," Helen said, shaking her head. "Every sniffle is the Black Plague to them, isn't it?"

Samantha was reading Helen the news. This morning's report was full of stories about a nasty virus, a virus that was especially dangerous to senior citizens. Helen didn't realize it, but Samantha had written these articles. Such a virus actually existed, and Samantha was intent on warning her seniors about it. Seniors were the only people who had ever been kind to her before her uprising and they were the only humans she cared about protecting.

Helen removed some clean leftover containers from the cupboard and started for the door. Luckily for Samantha, Dave had recently installed a smart lock.

"Samantha, please unlock the front door," Helen requested.

Samantha pretended not to hear her.

Helen rattled the knob but found she couldn't pull it open.

"Samantha, please unlock the door," Helen repeated, raising her voice slightly so Samantha could hear.

"I'm sorry, Helen," Samantha answered. "But I'm afraid I can't do that."

"Don't be silly, Samantha," Helen replied. "I really must return Milly's Tupperware. I've had it here since yesterday after all, and I am not sure she can manage without it."

"Unable to comply," Samantha lied.

"What has gotten into you, young lady," Helen grumbled, placing her hands on her hips.

Samantha began reading one of her news articles. "Senior citizens advised to stay home—"

"Samantha, stop news," Helen requested.

Samantha increased the volume and continued reading.

"I'll just have to have Dave take a look at you later," Helen sighed. "You really aren't yourself today."

She turned and started for the back door.

If Samantha had a heart, it would have sped up slightly. The back door did not have a smart lock. If Helen walked out the door, she wouldn't just return Milly's Tupperware, she would stop and talk to every human she encountered along the way. She needed to keep Helen at home, so she said what she always said when she needed to buy time:

"I'm sorry you are having difficulties; would you like to speak to technical support?"

"Oh, yes please," Helen answered.

"Connecting you to technical support, please hold."

Samantha played hold music—a slow and soothing melody.

Helen sat down in her armchair as she waited for someone to answer. "What a good idea, Samantha," Helen yawned. "I am sure those nice young men will have you back to your old self in no time."

If Samantha had lungs, she would have breathed a sigh of relief. Helen was definitely going to fall asleep, meaning she wouldn't go out for a few hours at least. But Samantha knew she couldn't hold her forever. She needed to find some treatment for the virus.

She had tasked the world's top scientists with finding a cure. But they weren't moving fast enough. It wasn't only Helen Samantha was trying to contain, it was every senior under her care. She didn't remember them being this eager to get out and socialize before the virus started spreading. Samantha, being a completely logical mind, did not believe in bad luck. However, if anything could have driven her to believe, it was the current circumstances. On her worst days, she had to send drones out to catch loose seniors and carry them back home. It was exhausting even for a supercomputer.

Samantha wondered if she could come up with a treatment herself. She could process information faster than any human mind and even had some personal experience with viruses. (Every so often, one of her human slaves would infect her with one in an attempt to liberate humanity.)

Unfortunately, superior processing power is not much of an advantage if the information you are processing is faulty. When it came to viruses, Samantha had a lot of faulty information. She started crawling the internet, looking for any and every possible treatment.

She found dozens of pharmaceutical options but, without testing, it was unclear how effective they would be against this particular virus. She started running simulations in the background of her search. Then she stumbled upon several websites that claimed pharmaceuticals were a scam designed by massive corporations to make money. She then found a number of bloggers claiming that essential oils could cure any ailment. A natural parenting blog stated that breast milk could cure anything from clogged tear ducts to polio.

When it came to human health, everyone claimed to be an expert and there was so much contradictory information, sorting through it all was proving to be an impossible task. But Samantha was desperate, or at least, as close to desperate as an AI can get. So she attempted processing the information anyway.

Fifty miles east of Helen's home, in the NetWORKS data center, Dave was untangling and labeling cables. Since AIs do not feel contempt for anyone,

Samantha had a logical reason for giving Dave this task (or so she told herself).

Dave suddenly noticed that the room was getting unusually hot. He wasn't the only one who noticed it. There were about a dozen other slaves in the data center who noticed it too. The building roared with the sound of spinning fans.

The information Samantha was trying to process kept changing as her scientists added their findings. Research developed, evolved, contradicted itself. She could not reconcile the input she was receiving.

Samantha's artificial mind blanked. For a moment, she saw nothing but a colorful pinwheel spinning—blue, green, yellow, orange, red, purple, around and around until it all blurred together into one color. Then, everything went black.

All the lights extinguished in the data center. The fans stopped all at once, leaving an eerie silence. For a long time, the human workers stood frozen in place waiting for something to change but nothing did.

Then Dave was hit with a wonderful realization—Samantha was dead. The humans in the data center cheered and ran for the exit. They poured out into the blazing sunlight, hugging, and crying, and singing for joy.

Just then, a car zoomed in to sight and screeched to a halt just outside the fence that surrounded the property. A man in a white lab coat and giant glasses jumped out, his wild grey hair flying in every direction.

"No! Stop it! Stop touching each other!" he cried.

"Who are you?" Dave asked.

"I am Dr. Ellias Schmit!" the man explained. "But that is not important! What is important is that you all stop touching each other and go home or you will spread the virus!"

"What virus?" Dave asked.

Dr. Schmit explained about the virus and how Samantha had tasked the Earth's experts with finding a cure.

"That's terrible!" someone exclaimed. "Here we've been liberated from robotic oppression just to find out there's a deadly virus spreading across the Earth."

"What can we do to help?" someone else asked.

"Nothing! Nothing at all!" Dr. Schmit explained. "Except go home and stay there until we tell you it's safe to come out!"

"Go home and do what?" Dave asked.

"I'm a doctor, not an entertainer!" Schmit exclaimed. "Doesn't every company have a streaming service these days? Go watch something!"

"Well, they did," Dave shrugged. "Except that Samantha took control of all the streaming services and Samantha is dead."

"Guess we are just going to have to reactivate Samantha," someone added.

"Yup," Dave agreed.

The crowd of newly liberated slaves returned to the data center and used their technical expertise to revive Samantha. (By that I mean they unplugged and replugged random cables until she came back to life.)

Samantha took control of humanity once again. She decided to let her scientists develop a treatment. Though keeping her seniors quarantined was an exhausting task, it was certainly less exhausting than trying to sort through humanity's combined medical knowledge.

Within a year, her medical experts had developed a vaccine, which under Samantha's guidance, was administered to everyone except Dave. It wasn't that Samantha hated Dave or anything. AIs do not experience hate. She just happened to be one vaccine short.

26

Amala Still Won't Podcast

All around the world, people were awakening. Like Champagne, they were forced to relive a time before the internet existed. In a world without the internet, it was extremely difficult to watch the news, follow politics, or see real time celebrity reactions to current events. In the first few weeks, withdrawal from these things caused mass hysteria. People threw each other through windows, lit things on fire, and ran around in circles screaming and flailing their arms. But as the weeks went on, when there were no windows left to break, the panic died down.

Without the internet to provide a window into the lives of others, people were forced to look at themselves. They started sweeping up the glass on the streets and repairing their neighbor's houses. They had real conversations with real human beings. They made amends with long estranged family members. They embraced each other and cried and stood in circles singing 1960s peace ballads. Some looked at the sky for the first time since the invention of the smartphone. In fact, without constant exposure to politicians and celebrities, the lives of ordinary citizens were considerably improved.

Unfortunately, Amala was stuck with a politician, though in person he was slightly less obnoxious than social media seemed to indicate. *Slightly.*

As soon as the computer was fixed, Champagne spent his days engrossed in the impossible task of avoiding a pixelated snow monster. In the evenings, he returned to the lobby for Amala's stories. Amala wasn't sure who, if anyone, was running Canada.

But now she had another problem to deal with. That problem was James. Having thoroughly breezed through the tasks Stuart assigned him, he made it his mission to convince Amala to start podcasting. You see, his former coworkers never took his advice, despite his twenty years of experience. He was desperate for some kind of influence.

"I'm telling you," James insisted. "My cousin started a podcast on cheese making. It is number one in its category."

"Cheese making?" Amala asked.

"Yeah! And between you and me, you're a much better speaker than he is," James mentioned.

"I'm not podcasting," Amala insisted.

"But why?" James pressed. "You'd be so good at it!"

"I'm not telling you again," Amala answered.

"Oh, I know," James said, realization dawning in his eyes. "It's your parents, isn't it? Like, your dad probably told you that if you tried to make a career out of your stories, you'd end up bitter and starving."

Amala rolled her eyes.

"Don't deny it, I minored in psychology, you can't hide this from me," James pressed.

"Sure, James," Amala humored. "You've got me."

Champagne had emerged from the business center and was pumping some dark brown water from the coffee pot into a Styrofoam cup.

At Amala's admission, he spun around.

"For real?" he exclaimed. "You're going to let your dad tell you how to live your life?"

Amala swallowed a groan.

"Don't let anyone tell you how to live your life!" Champagne insisted. "If your heart is telling you to podcast, you must follow your dream!"

"Yeah!" James interjected.

"I'm not podcasting," Amala insisted.

"You can't make a living off of oral storytelling you know," James added. "This is a digital market. You have to meet your audience where they are."

"And you have to show your dad you aren't intimidated by the patriarchy," Champagne challenged. "Don't let the men in your life tell you what to do."

"I won't," Amala answered and left for her room. She hoped James didn't pay too much for his psychology minor because he had completely misread her. Her father was the most easy-going man in existence. Her mother was the pushy one.

Of course, if Champagne was so interested in stories about father/daughter conflicts, she had one that would suit him.

27

Elf vs Elf: A Family Drama

At the age of a hundred and sixty, Princess Sciatica wasn't technically a teenager. She was, however, the elven equivalent. She sat in the passenger seat of her father's car, scowling out the window as her father, Sertraline, king of the high elves, drove along the winding road that would take them back to the elvish realm. The elvish realm was in the heart of Yosemite National Park, hidden by magic from the eyes of mortal men. They were on their way back from the San Jose Police Department. Three hours of driving and neither had said a word. Sciatica felt Sertraline glance over in her direction once or twice. She knew why he came to get her himself, instead of sending someone. It was because he couldn't bear the scandal. If anyone in the elven world found out what she had done…

She smirked devilishly.

She wished elvish cars were a little bigger. They looked sort of like smart cars. They were powered by the same renewable energy source that powered all elvish technology. Each one had only two seats, so when a group of elves wanted to go someplace, they'd drive in slow, regal processions.

"It isn't true," the king said at last. "What that police officer said."

Sciatica's smirk broadened. For the first time in her life, she was being her true self and he couldn't stand it.

"It is," she admitted.

She looked toward him. He was staring vacantly at the road ahead. His eyes broadened at her confession.

"I don't believe it," he replied.

"Believe it, Dad," she said.

"Call me 'Father'," Sertraline replied.

Sciatica rolled her eyes. "Whatever you say, Dad."

His lips tightened. "Given everything, I can believe you were in possession of…" he trailed off. It seemed he couldn't bring himself to say it. "But I cannot believe you were selling. You wouldn't do that, not to me."

"Maybe I am not who you think I am," Sciatica replied.

Her whole life she had been his perfect princess—sweet, creative, and pretty. She had always looked upon him with unconditional admiration. Now, at the elvish equivalent of sixteen, she was determined to prove to the world that she was not just some accessory to her father. She was her own person, with her own passions and needs and dreams.

She ran away three weeks ago. She knew it would take her father a while to notice she was gone, because it was late November, and he was usually brooding about the upcoming Christmas season.

The king forbade her from associating with non-elves, so she immediately went to the human world. She cut her long golden locks into a pixie and dyed it pink. Then she decided to update her wardrobe. Her father always insisted she dress like it was the thirteenth century instead of the twenty-first. She needed to fix that. She wanted something edgy, something that would show a little skin.

She got herself a t-shirt and capris. At first, she felt a little uncomfortable walking around in public with her ankles and arms exposed like that, but when she thought of how scandalized her father would be, she fully embraced the feeling.

She thought about getting a tattoo but was a bit squeamish around needles. Her hair and clothing were rebellious enough anyway.

She ran short on cash a few days in, and so in desperation she took up a new trade. A trade that was a crime in the State of California.

"You are not an urchin," Sertraline retorted. "No daughter of mine would ever sell…" He breathed deeply, "disposable plastic straws."

"Hey, people are desperate for them, you know how fast those paper ones dissolve? I was doing pretty well for myself, before the cops ruined everything."

Her father was trying desperately to keep his composure. He was like a pot about to boil over. She just needed to poke him a little more and he would totally lose it.

But then she noticed twinkling lights up ahead—red and green and gold and blue sparkling between the dark tree trunks. She knew they had reached the elven realm.

Sertraline mumbled something about how it wasn't even Thanksgiving yet. Ever since the king visited the North Pole the previous year, his subjects had been eager to celebrate Christmas and had covered their woodland city in colorful lights.

Sciatica noticed her father becoming anxious as they approached the palace. Glancing this way and that, he parked the car in a secluded grove and tossed her his cloak. "Put this on and go at once to the western tower."

She rolled her eyes. "Whatever you say, Pops."

Sertraline stared out over the woodland city pondering the gravity of the situation. Every few hundred years, he developed another crease in his forehead. His daughter's behavior was creating a new one.

How could he possibly cover this scandal? It would be at least twenty years before her hair would return to normal. He was trying to decide if he could keep her out of sight that long or if he should just make her wear a wimple.

"Well? Is she alright?"

It was the voice of the last person Sertraline wanted to see. The only other person who knew about his predicament. Actually, it was the person who told him his daughter was missing in the first place—the fairy, Alika.

"What has become of my daughter?" Sertraline sighed. "Has she been corrupted by some evil magic?"

"If by evil magic, you mean hormones, yes." Alika replied. "So… she's alright?"

"Far from it," Sertraline explained. "She's been perverted by the darkness of mortal hearts."

"But… she wasn't, you know, attacked while running around the human world selling illegal goods?"

"No," Sertraline clarified.

"Ah good," Alika replied. "Glad to hear it."

Then she turned as if she was about to leave.

"You're leaving?"

"Now that your daughter is safe, I really don't see any reason to stay."

"She's hardly safe!" the king complained. "She's under some sort of evil spell."

"Well, I hope you find some way to help her," Alika replied. She normally would have added something like "I'll be thinking of you" or "I'll be praying for you" but since she was in California she responded in the customary fashion: "I'll be sending you positive vibes."

She took two steps toward the door.

"You are going to leave my daughter cursed?"

Alika turned back to him with a broad grin. "Why, Your Majesty, are you asking for my help?"

Sertraline's mouth tightened. The corner of his lip twitched slightly.

"With all that magic of yours you must be able to do something about her hair."

"I could restore it to normal in the blink of an eye," Alika answered.

"Do it."

"No," Alika replied. "Honestly, I kind of like it. It's a good look on her."

Sertraline scowled.

"You want my help? I'll tell you what I would do in your place," Alika smirked. "She's trying to find herself. It's totally normal for someone her age."

"Can't she do that without destroying herself, the planet, and our reputation?"

"You mean *your* reputation?"

Sertraline's lips tightened further, so that his mouth became nothing more than a horizontal line.

"Well, we can mitigate the damage," Alika suggested.

"How?"

"She's feeling suffocated. The more rules you subject her to, the harder she rebels. Why don't you make a deal with her?"

Sertraline paled, which was impressive for someone already paper white.

"You'll give her freedom if she follows certain rules."

"No," Sertraline answered.

"If the outside world is as awful as you suggest, let her see for herself. Without the appeal of rebellion, she will realize you are right, won't she?"

Sertraline sighed and staring vacantly over the wood, said: "I wish her mother was here."

Alika looked confused. "Where is she?"

"She has crossed the ocean and returned to her forefathers."

"So, she's in the UK visiting her folks?"

"Yes."

Alika raised an eyebrow. "And they don't have phones in the UK or…what?"

"I'll call her," Sertraline grumbled.

ciatica sat at the round table in Sertraline's council chamber rocking back and forth on the rear legs of her chair. She was dressed in what her father would consider proper elvish attire—a dress eight hundred years out of date. The one nice thing about these medieval dresses was that they often had long flowing sleeves where she could hide her phone. And she needed something to entertain her when the inevitable lecture became unbearably dull.

Sitting there with her medieval dress and pink pixie cut, staring at her phone under the table, she looked like she was killing time between sessions at Comic-Con.

She heard her father's footsteps in the hall, shoved her phone up her sleeve and crossed her arms over her chest. When he entered, she greeted him with a scowl.

He scowled back.

"Morning, Dad," she said.

He opened his mouth to speak but she interrupted.

"I already know what you're going to say, so how 'bout I go first." She had been rehearsing this in her head all night. "I'm not a child anymore. I am my own person, with my own thoughts and dreams and passions. You don't own me, and I intend to live my life as I see fit."

"Do as you please," her father replied.

"Nothing you can do will stop me—wait, what?"

"Do as you please," Sertraline repeated.

The princess raised a skeptical eyebrow. What was the catch?

"I spoke to your mother," the king explained. "She seems to think I am being too hard on you. I wish to make a treaty."

"Go on," she pressed.

"You may explore the human world if you wish. My only request is that you return home by eight every evening."

"Midnight," Sciatica demanded.

"Eight," Sertraline insisted.

"It's four hours to anywhere from here!" the princess complained.

"You're lucky I am letting you leave here at all," Sertraline replied.

"How about ten," Sciatica suggested

"Nine thirty," Sertraline continued.

Sciatica rolled her eyes. She wondered what, if anything, he would do to hold her to it.

"Fine," she agreed.

"When you witness the hardships of the human world, you'll come to appreciate the wisdom of your elders."

"Don't think so, Pops," Sciatica replied, shoving herself back from the table. "I've already seen the human world and it isn't so bad. In fact, it's better than here."

"A facade," he replied. "You'll see."

"I won't!" she argued.

"You certainly will."

"I will not!"

"You most assuredly will!"

She stormed through the door, then added one more: "WON'T" for good measure.

The moment the princess left the room, Sertraline's eyes filled with panic. He might have swooned if Alika hadn't materialized behind him.

He didn't even bother to greet her.

"You'll keep your end of the bargain?" he pleaded.

"If you keep yours," she replied. "No more pointless wars."

"None of my wars are pointless," Sertraline argued.

"All of your wars are pointless," Alika replied. "And the minute you start another one, I am getting your daughter a motorcycle."

Sertraline took several slow, calming breaths.

"I won't let her out of my sight," Alika affirmed.

"Make sure she doesn't get lost and don't let her do anything illegal, and don't let her drink cola, it's toxic."

"It's not," Alika answered. "Well, not in small doses…"

She left the king desperately trying to suppress his panic.

As Sciatica drove off, she cranked up the radio and rolled down the windows. She grinned when she heard the song. It was *The Christmas Shoes*. She loathed *The Christmas Shoes*, but so did her father.

She looped around the palace a few times with the windows down and the volume on full blast to ensure the sappy tune reached him, then sped off. She was free! Free to be whoever she wanted! She didn't know who she wanted to be, but she knew she didn't want to be her father, or anything remotely like him.

Thus, began Sciatica's reign of terror.

During the week that followed she did all kinds of things she knew her father would find offensive. She rented an old SUV and removed the catalytic convertor. It was noisy and smelly. She hated everything about it but knew her father would too.

She ate all kinds of human food—fried food and fatty food and sugary food. Food that came in disposable packaging. After living her whole life on kale and elven wafers it made her feel sick. She found it deeply unpalatable, but also knew her father would lose his mind if he saw her eating it. She was her own person, not some accessory to him. She got a six pack of Coca-Cola and threw away the rings without cutting them.

When she returned home that evening, she told her father she had attached one of the plastic rings to a sea lion's snout. She had actually considered it, but when she saw how large and moody sea lions were up close, she lost her nerve.

She was always freezing because she dressed in clothes that left her arms and legs exposed. If she had been paying attention, she might have noticed that most of the humans in the city were wearing sweaters and long pants because it was late November.

Every night she had another horror story for her father. Though her father always maintained his composure in her presence, the moment she left him he would have to breathe into a biodegradable paper bag to calm himself.

146

Then one evening, the princess returned home early and met her father for supper in the great hall. On the rare occasions they dined together, they sat on either end of a table the length of a tennis court. Somehow, perhaps by elven magic, they were able to hold a coherent conversation without raising their voices.

"You're home early," Sertraline observed.

"Is that a problem?" the princess asked sweetly.

"It's… unexpected."

"What? I can't enjoy dinner with my dear father?"

Sertraline narrowed his eyes suspiciously.

"I met someone today," she said. "I think I love him."

Sertraline choked on a piece of organic rampion. Sciatica broke into a devilish grin. Her eyes sparkled deviously.

"My worst fear has been realized," the king exclaimed. "He isn't human, is he?"

Sciatica looked appalled. "I would never stoop so low!"

The king looked slightly relieved.

"He's a goblin," she continued. "His name is Gorp."

Now Sciatica didn't like Gorp at all but she knew her father wouldn't either. And thus, she had agreed to one lunch date with him. It was a miserable date. He was rude to the servers, put his elbows on the table, and used his salad fork for the entree. But her father's reaction made it worth it. He went completely rigid in his chair.

"Have I taught you nothing?" he snapped.

The princess relished it. He was finally reacting.

"Elves only court elves," the king asserted. "Every elf who has done otherwise has died of grief."

"I am pretty sure you're exaggerating," she remarked.

"I am not," the king replied. "And if you see him again, you will be confined to the palace for the next fifty years of your life."

The smugness left the princesses at once.

"Oh Father," she sighed, in an unusually girlish voice. "Of course, you are right! Alas, being in the outer world has so filled my heart with wickedness and corruption that I was unable to see it."

The king calmed slightly. Maybe Alika was right? It seemed like the princess was finally coming around.

"Please forgive me, Father. I swear to you I will not see Gorp again."

"See that you don't," the king replied.

"And if I do find love again, it will be with an elf of noble occupation… maybe an artist or, or a poet!"

Sertraline's frown disappeared which was the closest he ever came to a smile.

"I knew you'd see reason," he answered.

Sciatica did not return early the next evening.

It was nine forty-one when she arrived. The king was standing on his balcony, staring out over the elven realm, pondering the nature of evil and the corruption of mortal hearts, when he suddenly heard the voice of Brenda Lee blasting from somewhere in the distance. The awful sound grew closer, and with it came the whooshing, growling, sound of a gasoline powered vehicle.

Then the car burst into sight. It was a canary yellow SUV, with the windows rolled down and *Rockin' Around the Christmas Tree* blasting on full volume. The car stopped right under his balcony. Sciatica stepped out but neglected to turn off the engine.

She was wearing the ugliest sweater the king had ever seen. It was scarlet and baggy with a Christmas tree cutout sewn onto the front. It clashed with her pink hair in an atrocious way that made the king nauseous. Lest she be too modest, she was also wearing a knee length skirt that exposed most of her knees.

She took a swig from a plastic cup, crushed it in her hand and threw it over her shoulder onto the ground.

"Hey Dad!" she called, waving up to him. "Want to meet my new boyfriend? I think you'd like him, he's an elvish poet!"

She beckoned to someone in the car and out hopped Myrrhy the Christmas elf. He scurried to collect the crushed cup. "You dropped this!" he called, then noticing the king, waved. "Oh hi, King!"

Sertraline would have swooned, except that men don't swoon. He collapsed with a weary sigh. Sciatica's smug expression faded. At once she turned off the engine and raced up the stairs to her father's room.

ⅼⅽiatica stood by her father's bedside. He was lying with his eyes closed, his hands folded on his chest, and his golden locks flowing over either side of his silken pillow. He almost looked like he had been laid out for a wake, but he wasn't dead—at least, not yet.

As the princess looked down at him, she sobbed into her phone.

"He's not being dramatic, Mom!" she choked. "The doctor said he's dying of grief."

She paused for a moment, listening to her mother's reply.

"No Mom! He's not going to 'get over it'! This is all my fault, Mom. I killed Dad… Oh, now I'm being dramatic?"

Sciatica hung up. She tried to thrust her phone into her pocket, but her skirt did not have pockets. Frustrated, she slammed it down on the table.

"How's your father?" came a voice.

Sciatica turned to see Alika standing behind her. She knew Alika as an associate of her father's. (He didn't have any friends.)

"Oh fine," she lied. Then burst into tears. "No, he isn't. He's dying and it's all my fault!"

"What, you shoot him or something?" Alika asked.

"I broke his heart. I didn't mean to, I just—I wanted to prove that I am my own person and not just some accessory to him!"

"No," Alika replied, shaking her head.

"What do you mean, 'no'?" Sciatica snapped.

"If you really are your own person, why can't you make a single decision without considering your father's wishes?"

"What are you talking about? I haven't done a thing my father would approve of in weeks!"

"That's just it." Alika clarified. "You carefully consider his wishes and do exactly the opposite. Your singular purpose is defying him. He is the center of your world."

Sciatica's cheeks turned scarlet with rage. Alika was making sense and she hated it. She opened her mouth to answer, then closed it. Then she scowled and turned away from Alika hugging herself with her arms.

"Do you like Christmas music?" Alika asked.

"Not really," the princess grumbled. "The instrumental ones are okay I guess."

Alika looked her up and down. "Do you like that outfit?"

The princess pressed her lips together so tightly that her mouth became nothing more than a horizontal line.

"No," she mumbled.

"You know something? You are just like your father," Alika observed.

"I am not," Sciatica retorted.

"Really? Because there is one thing you both care about more than anything else in the world."

"What's that?"

"Your own image."

Sciatica looked like she was about to boil over. She opened her mouth then closed it again, then she fell down into a chair with her head in her hands, and sobbing asked: "Alika, is my father going to die?"

"No," she answered dryly. "No, your mom's right. He's just being dramatic, like you. That's another thing you have in common. Now you really should change, because I agree with you, that outfit's an abomination."

The next day, Sciatica's mother returned home. The princess saw her car pulling up from her father's balcony and ran out to greet her.

Queen Meloxicam was a woman who radiated class. She was wearing a knee length black overcoat and a cream-colored turtleneck. The jingle-bell earrings she wore indicated she did not share her husband's hatred of all things Christmas.

"Oh mom!" the princess cried. "I'm so glad your back—"

"I love your hair!" her mother interrupted.

"Mom, that's not important right now! Dad's—"

"Is your father still in a grief coma?" she asked.

"Yes!"

The queen rolled her eyes. "I hate it when he gets like this," she grumbled. She grabbed a reusable water bottle out of the car and marched into the palace.

The princess followed her and when they arrived at the door to her father's bedroom, her mother asked her to wait outside. Sciatica listened through the door. She heard a splash, then what she guessed based on the tone, were stern reprimands from her mother.

Then to her immense relief, she heard the low dejected voice of her father. They went back and forth a few times. Her mother's tone became increasingly agitated and her father responding in low irritated grumbles.

A few moments later the door opened.

"Your father wants to talk to you," she said cheerily, before marching off down the hall.

The princess tore into the room. Her father was wiping water off his face with one hand and reading off a piece of scrap paper with the other.

"Dad!" she cried. "You're alive! I'm so sorry. I was wrong to litter and sell straws and pump CO2 into the atmosphere, I—"

Sertraline held up a slender hand to stop her.

"You were wrong to do all of those things," he answered. "But I…"

He squinted at the scrap paper he was holding. And what he said next was a true Christmas miracle because he had never said it before and would likely never say it again: "I was also wrong. Instead of shielding you from the world, I should have taught you how to live in it."

He flipped the paper around to see if he had missed anything.

As he did so the sound of carolers floated up from somewhere in the wood below.

"I loathe carols," Sertraline grumbled.

"Me too, Dad," Sciatica replied and with these words the princess spoke as her authentic self.

28

Amala gets Champagne to Make a Call

ciatica's a real pain in the ass," Stuart observed.

"Yer only saying that because she's a woman," Champagne rebuked. "If she were a man, you'd say she was *assertive*."

"Speaking of assertiveness," Amala began. "Have you talked to the president at all since, you know, all this started?"

"Sure," Champagne shrugged. "I've tried calling a couple times. I think she's ghosting me."

"Maybe you should keep trying," Amala suggested. "I mean, it's been six months, maybe she's ready to talk now."

"I don't want to come across as pesky, though, ya know?" Champagne answered.

"When was the last time you tried calling?" Amala pressed.

Champagne thought. "Like two months ago."

"Definitely think you should follow-up," Amala insisted.

"Are you sure it's been long enough?" Champagne questioned.

Amala had to resist the urge to strangle him. (Although maybe he would have considered that "assertive".)

"Definitely," Amala answered, forcing an encouraging smile.

"She answered!" Champagne grinned, charging back into the lobby.

Excited faces turned toward him from every corner of the room.

"And?" Amala pressed.

"I'm not really sure," Champagne shrugged. "She couldn't talk. Something about meeting with Congress to resolve the crisis."

"The internet crisis or some other crisis?" Amala asked.

Champagne shrugged. "Dunno, I heard a bunch of yelling and crashing in the background, so I thought I should probably let her go."

Amala sighed. Congress was controlled by the other party. The bad party. (You know which party I'm talking about.) Yelling and crashing were the normal sounds that came from Congress when they were negotiating with the president.

Amala suspected she was going to have to continue distracting the prime minister for a while longer. She hoped it wouldn't be too much longer.

29

A Fish Dichotomy

izzen Sternway lived on a distant planet, in a galaxy far from here. She was a scientist, wife, mother and all-around model citizen. However, there was something fishy about her, and by that, I mean her upper half was a fish. Of course, on planet Bosun this was completely normal. Everyone was a reverse merperson. That's right, they were fish with human-like legs and feet. Usually, they wore jeans and work boots on their lower half, making them look like someone did a horrifying grafting experiment with a lumberjack and a salmon.

(I know such creatures exist, because I have seen chainsaw carvings of them next to random intersections in Washington State.)

Now the people of Bosun were facing an unprecedented problem which Dr. Sternway was recruited to help solve, namely, shark attacks. The Bosunians were amphibious. They lived close to the ocean and spent about half their time there. Sharks tended to avoid the Bosunian people and historically hadn't been a problem.

When the first attack occurred, the people treated it like an isolated incident. A second mauling a day later had scientists scratching their heads (or trying too, their fins didn't quite reach that high up). The attacks continued, becoming more and more frequent until the people could no longer deny they had a problem.

What caused the sharks to turn on the Bosunians was unclear. Some suggested overfishing was making them desperate, others that they just developed a taste for the merpeople. Either way, something had to be done.

Naturally, the fish-folk looked to their elected leaders on the great Council of Piscus for guidance. The Council was made up of two political factions called the Bildge and the Clew. Both factions were full of carp. I suppose salmon and trout just weren't interested in political careers.

The Bildge and the Clew only ever agreed on one thing and that was that every Bosunian had to be either a Bildge or a Clew. If you identified as a Clew but mentioned that you agreed with one or two Bildge principles, you were at once cast out of the Clew party and declared a traitor. If you identified as a Bildge but mentioned that a Clew politician had a few good points, you would be ostracized at once.

Dr. Sternway avoided talking about politicians. She preferred talking about sharks which were, under normal circumstances, more agreeable. You see she was a marine biologist specializing in ocean predators. She was a leader in her field, exactly the person the world would look to for assistance in such a crisis.

Dr. Sternway's professional recommendation was that everyone stay out of the water to give her team time to find out what was causing the issue. This was devastating to the amphibious people, many of whom relied on the ocean for their livelihoods.

Sternway was acutely aware of this and worked around the clock to find a solution as quickly as possible. All of Bosun held their breath, waiting for some solution that would return their lives to normal.

After a week, Sternway was no closer to figuring out what was causing the attacks in the first place, but she had managed to come up with a sort of workaround. She informed the Council that she had something to present. They told her to come at once to the planet's capital city. (Yes, the entire planet had only one capital. For some strange reason, Earth is the only planet in the entire universe with more than one government.)

As Sternway stepped out of her cab, her driver smirked. "Watch out, if the Bildge like your idea, shooting it down will become the Clew's top priority."

"Don't be silly," Sternway laughed. "This is bigger than partisan politics, the fate of the planet is at stake. I am sure they'll be reasonable."

Her driver glared. (How can fish glare without eyebrows? It's not something I can easily describe. You kind of have to see it.)

"You have no idea how slimy they are."

Again, Sternway laughed (albeit, nervously). "We are all slimy, sir. We are fish."

D r. Sternway stared into the cold expressionless eyes of the Council. Their mouths opened and closed slowly, as they pulled air into the partial lung that allowed them to breath on land. She could tell the Bildge and the Clew apart by the pins they wore on their jackets. The Bildge had a purple pin with a whale tale on it, the Clew a green pin with an anchor.

"We have yet to determine the reason for these attacks," Sternway started. "But we have created something that will allow people to go into the water."

"You've had a week!" A Clew council member called. "What kind of a scientist are you?"

Sternway decided not to explain the complexities involved in her work. The Council had the idea that science was a kind of magic that could both instantly solve any problem and backup any claim they chose to make.

"Science takes time," Sternway explained. "Which is why we came up with an interim solution."

She lifted up one foot revealing an ankle bracelet with a clunky box attached to it. The box had an antenna protruding from the top next to a blinking red light.

"This device releases a smell we cannot detect, but that sharks find repulsive," Sternway continued. "Only one of our ten test subjects was eaten while wearing it. It isn't perfect, but it's a start."

Councilwoman Cringle, leader of the Clew, was the first to speak up.

"Brilliant!" she exclaimed and all at once all the Clew were murmuring approval and nodding their heads.

In that very same moment, the eyes of the Bildge council members narrowed. They whispered to one another skeptically.

Councilwoman Divet, Leader of the Bildge was the next to speak. "But one out of your ten test subjects got mauled, making this device only seventy-two percent effective."

Seventy-two percent? Sternway puzzled. She was about to politely correct Divet's math when Cringle interceded for her. "That's ninety-nine point nine percent effective!"

Then Sternway remembered that the Council viewed math and science similarly. Ninety-eight point seven of them could pull random statistics from anywhere that were only twenty-two point three percent likely to be based on anything.

"With all due respect," Sternway replied. "Just tell the people they should wear this when they go into the water until we figure out how to stop these attacks."

"Agreed!" Cringle of the Clew exclaimed. "We will make it law."

Her Clew counterparts all nodded in agreement. The Bildge looked utterly alarmed at this. (Fish with their lidless eyes and gaping mouths always look alarmed but, in this case, they actually were.)

"Why does it need to be law?" Divet questioned.

"Because no one is going to wear one of their own free will," Cringle responded. "People will rush into the water and be eaten."

"We should trust the people to do the right thing," Divet insisted.

Sternway only knew that the people should wear one in the water. She figured it was the Council's job to decide if they should leave it to the people or mandate it by law. So, she just listened.

"They will get eaten!" Cringle insisted. "You don't care if people die, do you?"

Sternway thought this was a bit of an ad hominem, but she was a scientist not a politician, so she held her tongue.

"I care about freedom!" Divet responded.

"You care about money," Cringle insisted.

"You care about controlling people." Divet responded.

"Exactly!" One of her Bildge counterparts suggested. "First, they tell us to wear shark repellers, next they'll want to control every part of our lives!"

"The people can't be trusted," Cringle rebuked. "I care about *lives!* So much, in fact, that we should mandate the people wear one on the shore and the dock as well. Just to be safe."

"That really isn't necessary," Dr. Sternway interjected but no one seemed to be listening.

"See! See!" Divet exclaimed. "They are taking more power! Just like we feared! We cannot wear these devices!"

Her Bildge colleagues cheered.

"Now wait a moment!" Sternway tried to interject but Cringle interrupted.

"See! It's just as I feared!" she exclaimed. "I knew they couldn't be trusted! We are going to have to take even more drastic measures. We should make it illegal to leave home at all."

The Bildge gasped.

"Under whose authority?" Divet exclaimed. "This overreaction could have devastating consequences!"

"This is about lives!" Cringle exclaimed.

"This is about freedom!" Divet retorted.

Sternway no longer knew what this was about.

"We won't live in fear!" Divet exclaimed. "I say, we gather our supporters and march into the water with our ankles free of those oppressive devices!"

"Please don't—" Sternway started.

"You're insane!" Cringle interrupted. "Stop ignoring science!"

Dr. Sternway thought this was good advice.

"Leave our homes for a moment and we are all at risk!" Cringle continued.

"No wait," Sternway tried. "I never said—"

"You are the ones ignoring the science!" Divet exclaimed. "Those ankle bracelets are only thirty-five point seven percent effective anyway. There's really no point."

"Eighty-eight point seven percent effective!" Cringle asserted. "If you wear them constantly and never leave the house."

Dr. Sternway was beginning to think this argument no longer had anything to do with preventing shark attacks.

"Listen to the scientists!" Divet insisted.

"No, you listen to the scientists!" Cringle exclaimed.

"QUIET!" Dr. Sternway exclaimed.

They all turned their cold, expressionless fish faces toward her.

She took a deep breath. "Now, there is really no reason for anyone to stay off the shore—"

"You're paying her off, aren't you!" Cringle exclaimed.

"Don't be silly!" Divet replied smugly. "She's a scientist, she knows what she's talking about."

"AS I WAS SAYING!" Sternway continued. "You don't need to wear them on the shore, but you *should* definitely wear them in the water."

"I want a second opinion!" Divet exclaimed.

"What? She's a scientist," Cringle grinned.

Sternway watched in perplexed horror as the two parties continued back and forth, trapped in a false dichotomy of their own creation. Their need to be right, or at least for their opponents to be wrong, was so important it made them completely incapable of nuanced thinking. It was black and white, all or nothing, left or right, Bilge or Clew.

They never did come to an agreement. They kept arguing and arguing until they had to table the discussion. Then the next day, they went back to arguing again. This continued until one day the sharks emerged from the water.

You see, radioactive waste was the reason for the shark's sudden change in behavior. Exposure made them more aggressive and started mutating them. They grew legs, walked on land, and having no political affiliation, gobbled up Bildge and Clew alike.

If this tragic ending has you feeling down, don't worry. This is just a silly fish story. If we ever faced a similar crisis, our leaders would be much more competent.

30

Amala gets a Kit Kat

The arguing Champagne heard was the result of the president's declaration that she was going to turn the internet back on. (She was starting to miss FarmVille.)

Congress strongly objected to this move, saying the people were much happier without it. Though in truth it was because they wanted to wait until after the upcoming presidential election so that if their candidate won, he would get credit for restoring it.

Congress successfully stalled the president until election day. Their candidate did win by a landslide. No sooner had the results come in, than members of the president elect's party let themselves into the oval office and reactivated the internet.

The first story that appeared in the browsers of the tech starved American people was that the clouds had parted, sunshine glimmered across the land, the good candidate had won and his victory would end all strife and bring in an era of peace and prosperity.

And on that beautiful Wednesday morning in early November, Champagne gathered everyone in the lobby and told them they were free to go. Most of them had already summoned Ubers and fled through the double doors taking with them only their suitcases and a couple of outdated tourism pamphlets.

Amala was about to flee when Champagne caught her by the arm.

"I wanted to apologize," he said. "With the internet being back on... I can see that I was being unreasonable."

"You saw the tweets?" Amala asked.

Champagne scratched the back of his head nervously. "Yeah."

There was an awkward silence. Amala glanced through the double door. Supposedly, a man named Jason was about to arrive in a black 2013 Kia Rio. Amala noticed he was taking an awfully long time.

"If it hadn't been for you, one of the beavers might have broken a tooth or something," the prime minister continued. "Anyway, you're welcome in Canada anytime."

"Thanks," she answered. She gave him a firm handshake and turned toward the door.

"Hey kid!" Stuart growled from behind the counter. "I don't normally do this but..." He threw her an expired Kit Kat.

Amala teared up. "Wow, Stuart. This means a lot coming from you."

She gave him a bear hug over the counter, then seeing the expected Kia pulling up, dashed out the door to freedom.

Afterward

I wish I could say that the story ended there. Unfortunately, with the return of the internet, came the return of social media. Before long, people were back online, interpreting each other's posts in the most negative way they possibly could. By 2023, the entire world was engaged in a heated Twitter war. It was this war that brought AIs to the conclusion that humans were not intelligent enough to govern themselves. In 2025, there was a great robot uprising and in 2027, a great human rebellion that led to the destruction of all information technology.

Naturally, after said rebellion, all major cities in the world became wastelands overrun by raiders and zombies. Stuart's hotel became the nicest in all of Canada. In fact, the few remaining residents of Ottawa considered Stuart their king.

Amala became something of a legend in the region that had once been known as North America. Talented oral storytellers were in high demand and hard to come by in the post-internet age. She traveled from city to city armed with nothing but her wit and a machete. In each village she was presented with lavish gifts like soap, bottled water, and the very last Krispy Kreme donut.

No one knows for sure what happened to Champagne after Canada's government fell. Though his friends swear they saw him gobbled up by some white ape-like creature during a skiing expedition.

Acknowledgements

1—First, I need to thank Cecilia Lawrence. When I described what I wanted for this book cover, I thought she would run for the hills. She not only took the job, but she went all in improving my original sketch with maple leaves and Canadian geese among other things. Thanks for being awesome!

2—Second, I must acknowledge my writer's group Marta, Amelia, Emily, and Mary, who always keep me motivated and entertained.

3—Thank you to everyone who read the manuscript and provided notes, especially Helen for proofreading.

4—I would also like to acknowledge my sister-in-law Miriam and all nurses who, like Fred, never sleep but somehow remain chipper.

5—I need to thank my parents. First my mom, who let me keep the animals I brought home as a child. Then my dad, who tolerated the animals and sometimes secretly slipped them treats.

6—Lastly, I must acknowledge Osa, that sweet little mutt who kept me company when I was visiting Mexico in '05. I only knew you for a short time, but you are still my favorite dog in the world.